Towards Women's Liberation

Towards Women's Liberation: The Novels of Ashapurna Devi and Sulekha Sanyal

R. Mridula

Prestige
an international publishing house

Published by

Prestige Books International

New Delhi 110060

prestigebooks@gmail.com

ISBN: 978-81-922089-4-7

Printed at Chaman Offset Printers, Delhi

Contents

Contents

Chapter I

Introduction

Regional writing in India has a long and proud history. The texts, in different regional languages of India, document the writers' engagements with the social, cultural, and political forces which created the milieu within which they articulated their contentions. The developments in the literary spaces of Bengal on which this study focuses, image the indomitable human will that drives the oppressed on to challenge the societal prescriptions that paralyze them and to create a new system where they can live as complete, independent subjects.

Bankim Chandra Chatterjee's *Durgesh Nandini*, published in 1864, marked the beginning of a rich tradition of fiction in Bengal. In the twentieth century, when Bengal entered a turbulent phase in its history, powerful writers like Rabindranath Tagore (1861-1941) Saratchandra Chatterjee (1876-1938), Bibhutibhushan Bannerjee (1894-1950), Tarashankar Bannerjee (1898-1971), and Manik Bannerjee (1908-1956) made their signatures and laid out a ground that was to be elaborated through the latter decades of the century. They were the best chroniclers of the time and wrote about the rising nationalism, the decline and decay of the feudal fabric, the tensions between the rural and urban ways of life, and the conflict between tradition and modernity. In their works the traditional systems of life became sites of cultural contention.

These writers were definitely the harbingers and the historians of change. But the reworking of the world, in their fiction, was caste- and class-oriented. Gender was not as seriously debated as class and caste. The endeavours of men to transcend the limits imposed on them by the society, which was controlled by dominant classes and castes, were acknowledged and applauded. But women's attempts to challenge oppressions and to attain personhood were either completely ignored or only partially documented.

While these narratives of reform, resolution and liberation formed the core of the literary creativity of the time, alternative discourses were taking shape at the margins. The women writers, who were contemporaries of the male writers mentioned, drew upon the same social and cultural milieu, but with a major difference. They perceived the world around them through the eyes of the woman and articulated their responses and resistance from their decentred positions. As Susie Tharu and K. Lalitha, in their introduction to *Women Writing in India*, suggest:

> Familial ideologies, for instance, clearly constitute male and female subjectivities in different ways, as do ideologies of nation or of empire. Further, ideologies are not experienced—or contested—in the same way from different subject positions. . . . If we restrain ourselves from enthusiastically recovering women's writing to perform the same services to society and to nation that mainstream literature over the last hundred years has been called upon to do, we might learn to read compositions that emerge from these eccentric locations in a new way; we might indeed learn to read them not for the moments in which they collude with or reinforce dominant ideologies of gender, class, nation or empire, but for the gestures of defiance or subversion implicit in them. (35)

The narratives of the women writers confronted and documented those aspects of a woman's life which were earlier invisibilised as too embarrassing to recognize and reaffirmed the validity of woman's experience. Their fiction can, thus, rightly be considered as critiques of the structures of domination that determined the lives of women and as honest representations of individual and collective transcendence to personhood.

The most powerful articulations of a womanist ontology in Bengali literature can be seen in Ashapurna Devi (1909-1995), the first woman writer in India to win the *Jnanpith.* Her trilogy, *Pratham Pratishruti, Subarnalatha,* and *Bakulkatha,* records the dreams and aspirations of women who were inmates of the dark antahpurams and motivate the women of the new generations to remember the heroic struggles of their foremothers who fought to help woman actualize her potential personhood. She had, at the time when she started writing, the much trodden path of 'anatomizing oppression' (*Of Woman Born* 84) open before her. But she strode down the untrodden path to write about the women who broke the silence.

Modern critics and scholars acknowledge the strong feminist content in her narratives and welcome them as powerful female bildungsromans. Traditionally, the bildungsroman is a male affair because as Louise. F. Caton observes, it "has a perceived history of only turning the boy into the man, not the girl into the woman." (*Romantic Struggles* 126) Ashapurna Devi redefines the bildungsroman as the growing up story of a girl who is determined to envision and reach selfhood. She establishes that the life of the female is not always shadowed by uncertainties and inconclusiveness and that a woman's story need not always end in defeat. She very successfully constructs images of transcendence and authenticity for women.

Pratham Pratishruti, Subarnalatha and *Bakulkatha* are indeed systematic assertions of female, ontological transcendence to personhood. But labelling them merely as bildungsromans limits the infinite possibilities of the texts because they are much more than that. The convergence of the overtly contradictory notions of autonomy and community makes these novels extremely important. In her seminal work, the trilogy, Ashapurna Devi traces the female protagonists' quest for subjecthood, but with an important difference. Her protagonists, women who successfully transcend to personhood, are willing to address and attend to difference. The imaginative power of the writer juxtaposes each person's separate values and interests into a common collective pool of love, caring and sharing. Ashapurna Devi argues for women's groups of a permanent kind and against each woman going adrift in her own delicate little boat. She says, "Women need a special kind of self-sufficiency which can come only with the consolidation of female power." (*Indian Women* 22) So her women characters reach across caste and class to help each other actualize their potential. Satyabati, Subarna, and Bakul are autonomous subjects and are capable of steering the course of their lives, but that does not make them solitary individuals. They are in perfect communion with their collective and their relationship with the same sex collective is marked with mutual understanding and friendship. Thus Ashapurna Devi opens up the possibility of a different paradigm by suggesting that a common forum, where women are placed in relational, interlocutory dimensions, can be created.

Sulekha Sanyal (1928-1962) has two novels, *Nabankur* (1956) and *Dewal Padma* (1964) and a collection of short stories, *Sindure Megh,* to her credit. She did not receive the critical acclaim she so richly deserved during her life time, and even now readers of Bengali literature are not as familiar with her creative work as they are with Ashapurna Devi's. But the serious work of feminist thinkers and academics, aimed at writing a feminist literary history and locating a female tradition of writing which has long been neglected, has retrieved her works from the margins and has opened up the possibilities of analysis and discussions. Susie Tharu and K. Lalitha observe:

> in each of her remarkable books, one is brought face to face with the torment of human beings living through one of the most difficult phases of Bengal's history—the famine of the forties, the partition at Independence, and the consequent disintegration of the society they [Bengali women] were familiar with. This is the world Sulekha Sanyal's women live and fight in. (291)

Her narratives develop in the open, troubled world of socio-political unrest and in the process, pull down the barriers between the personal and the political. The emerging modernity and social crisis lead to the weakening of the absolute power of the brahmin patriarch. In her novel, *Nabankur*, the female protagonist is a rebel and, poignantly, a winner. The other women, initially, find it difficult to understand her attempts to assert her identity but later they help the little birdling grow her wings and fly away to freedom. The growth of the individual becomes the growth of the collective also.

Sanyal's creative genius includes political and economic slavery as a thematic concern in her fiction but it remains as a subtext while the 'woman issue' forms the core. The gender issue is the most seriously debated aspect in her works, even though she allows other social issues to intersect it. Her primary concern, like Ashapurna Devi's, is with the individual's and the collective's attempts to actualize their potential.

In the narratives of Ashapurna Devi and Sulekha Sanyal, one can see the ancient concepts of *dynamis* and *entelecheia* functioning as unique correlative principles that establish a cathexis between women and selfhood. Aristotle in his *Metaphysics* examines the concepts of *dynamis* (potentiality) and *entelecheia* (actuality) and argues that the being that can move and therefore change always bears with in it the origin of movement or *dynamis*. This origin then passes over to the actual movement or *entelecheia*. Thus movement and change are possible only because they actualize what lies already dormant and waiting to be actualized. When a woman becomes a subject, there is an ontological transcendence from potentiality to actuality. The urge for personhood is latent in her consciousness but patriarchal norms create an impasse making the process of subjectification difficult. Dominant, patriarchal, dualistic thoughts on male-female equation are informed by certain sets of polarities like spirit-matter, reason-emotion and subject-object. Such polarizations define women as fragmented, incomplete and inferior beings. The women who are potential subjects challenge the polarities, surmount the impasse and succeed in becoming complete persons.

A unified sensibility, which is a synthesis of feeling and thought, emotion and reason, is the primary requisite of the potential subjects. The perceptions of such women can integrate intelligence and experience, reason and suffering. Unlike the large majority in their same-sex collective, they reflect on the socio-cultural injustices that problematise their lives and engage with them actively. While the unawakened women suffer, internalize and naturalize victimization unthinkingly, the women endowed with the unified sensibility recreate their feelings in thoughts. Thus the experience of suffering and the spontaneous resistance to it merge to become the *dynamis* that will evolve into *entelecheia* and initiate their transformation from potential to actual persons.

But personhood is not the objective and achievement of the privileged few alone. The subjecthood of the woman is sharpened and intensified when it is brought into contact with her collective. Her subjectivity is marked by utter selflessness and at its highest point it becomes completely objective. She becomes an integral part of her community, the community of women. Her presence is a source of inspiration to the unawakened masses and causes more persons to be born. Thus the spiritual and psychological development corresponds with empowerment and liberation at the personal and collective levels.

Women authors like Ashapurna Devi and Sulekha Sanyal believe that the woman who transcends to personhood is sculpted by many women. Their narratives reclaim the importance of affiliations which have been lost through the traditional logic of identity. The themes and nuances are surprisingly ahead of their time and the core texts encode the conviction that the social possibilities and cultural assertions of the Achiever Woman emerge from the psychic osmosis between the woman and her collective. The pivotal textual strategy that makes these novels perennially relevant is the ideology of woman bonding posited as a metaphor of holistic health.

Woman bonding, as an ideology and practical necessity, is one of the most widely debated topics in feminist academic circles across the globe. Ashapurna Devi and Sulekha Sanyal conceptualize woman bonding as a strategy of survival and empowerment. Their novels document the trajectories of individual women's lives, which intersect with the history of social change. This documentation is complete, well-knit and has an organic unity because it touches upon all the four stages of transition and progress. In their works, the female protagonist, who attains personhood does not remain a privileged, singular individual and is not alienated from her society. At the height of her subjecthood, she is superbly selfless and considers the awakening and empowerment of her collective as more important than personal happiness. She includes the community in her dreams and aspirations. The collective reciprocates by appreciating her efforts, offering moral support and by willingly allowing her to mould them. From this solidarity there arises the consequent socio-cultural transformation. This recurrent narrative pattern is prominently present in Ashapurna Devi's trilogy, *Pratham Pratishruti*, *Subarnalatha*, *Bakulkatha* and Sulekha Sanyal's *Nabankur: The Seedling's Tale*. They tell us stories of the mother-daughter dyad, of kinship relations, of loving bonds that embrace the whole community of women. They show that bonding among same sex collective is successful in bringing about changes. Thus their novels valorize woman bonding and validate the practicality of it.

It is extremely important that even though their protagonists are upper caste, kulin brahmin women, they have a complete disregard for caste and initiate friendships with women of other castes. Solidarity among women thus becomes a viable strategy to create more persons who can challenge the dominant power structures and bring about sustentative changes in the condition of women.

Female relationships, in the empirical and fictional dimensions, have always been discredited and ignored as an impossibility. Man, cross-culturally, accepts the ideology of solidarity as a strategy of empowerment and survival but he perceives the relationships among women as an absence. The attempt of women to commune with each other is often treated with suspicion and contempt. Nina Auerbach observes: "The initiation into a band of brothers is a traditional privilege symbolized by uniforms, rituals, and fiercely shared loyalties; but sisterhood often looks like a blank exclusion." (*Communities of Women* 1). Adrienne Rich locates the reason for this male contempt in fear: "This is the real separation they dread—that women should not be waiting for them when they return from the male group, the hierarchies, the phallic world." (*Of Woman Born* 213). This fear drives the male to design clever, cruel, tools to fracture and fragment the relationship among women. Male supremacist ideology encourages women to believe that they obtain value only by maintaining their relationships with men and that female relationships diminish rather than enrich their experience. They are further taught that women are relational enemies and that solidarities will never exist between them.

Down the centuries, women have learned this lesson, without daring to articulate the obvious questions, but now they are unlearning it. They are trying to learn the true meaning and value of woman bonding. They are opening their eyes to the eternal truth that bonding is self-healing.

Fragmentariness and the resulting loneliness can jeopardize a woman's attempt to attain autonomy, and the problem can be resolved only with the help of a new strategy—a strategy that subsumes a new ethics. Hence Julia Kristeva's concept of herethics gains centrality in any discourse of woman bonding and empowerment. In her famous essay, "Stabat Mater," Kristeva introduces her concept: "Now, if a contemporary ethics is no longer seen as being the same as morality; if ethics amounts to not avoiding the embarrassing and inevitable problematics of the law but giving it flesh, language and jouissance—in that case its reformulation demands the contribution of women . . . of mothers" (*The Kristeva Reader* 185). This is the outlaw's ethics or heretical ethics and she calls it herethics. It challenges the existing, androcentric ethics, which is based on restriction and repression. Kelly Oliver suggests, "Herethics sets up one's obligations to the other as obligations to the self and obligations to the species. This ethics binds the subject to the other through love and not law." (*Ethics, Politics and Difference in Julia Kristeva's Writing* 5).

To Kristeva, the model of ethical love is the mother's love for the child which is a love for herself and a love for her own mother. She believes that motherhood needs the support of a mother's mother and that the mother's oscillating union/ disunion with her child recalls her own union with her mother. She opens a discourse on motherhood, which is not based upon woman's repudiation of the other women, of her mother, and seeks the possibility of relation to our mothers as singular subjects, located in their specificity, their difference from the absolute woman: "By giving birth, the woman enters in to contact with her mother; she becomes, she is her own mother; they are the same continuity differentiating itself." (*Desire in Language* 239). A mother's love thus, is not a powerful torrent that gushes forward to engulf the child. It is a current that flows in different directions, reaching back to the earlier and reaching out to the future generations. Jung stresses this continuity when he says: "Every mother contains her daughter within herself and every daughter her Mother. . . . Every woman extends backwards into her mother and forwards into her daughter. . . . The conscious experience of these ties produces the feeling that her life is spread out over generations" (*Essays on a Science of Mythology* 162). This love which is a continuum is constructive because it respects identity as well as alterity. In the absence of oppressive, unidirectional love, matricidal drive becomes non-existent. This mother-daughter dyad forms the core of kinship and communal relationships.

The strong mother, a woman with perceptions and priorities, does not demand her child's identity to be subsumed in her's and does not weave her daughter's life into monotonous, unchanging patterns. But autonomy is not the only lesson that the daughter learns. The daughter brought up by the strong mother imbibes another, equally important truth. She learns respect for alterity. She accepts that she is not the sole object of her mother's desire. They are two beings, located in their specificity and have the space to grow and experience healthy companionship. The semiotic, material remains as a permanent trace in the daughter's subjectivity and makes an ethical orientation possible. Nancy Chodorow observes that the daughter's "experience of self contains more flexible or permeable ego boundaries" (*Reproduction of Mothering* 169). The female sense of self connects her to the others in the world. Relationships thus come to mean plurality, continuity, inter-dependence and jouissance.

The mothering theories of the writers mentioned above, especially Kristeva's theory of herethics, thus make a paradigmatic shift from the ethics of identity to the ethics of alterity. Her ideology of selfhood does not privilege individuality and separateness over community. But to get at the right nuance of the term community, when used by Kristeva, we should be aware of the conceptual revision that takes place. She subverts the established hierarchies when she says, "The community of women is a community of dolphins." (*Kristeva Reader* 181). It is not the silent, unnamable community where silent, passive women, mere objects, huddle together. It is a community where each woman is a subject with an awakened self. But instead of the 'war of singularities' (182), there is an open-minded acceptance. Plutarch has observed that nature has given to the dolphin alone something which the best philosophers seek, friendship for no advantage. It is this selfless bonding based on the herethics of love that makes individual and collective growth possible.

Of course this collectivity is not an undifferentiated fusion where woman disappears. Differences are acknowledged, but the other is loved and womanhood is celebrated. It is an ethical approach where ethics is the recognition of the primacy of alterity over identity. Isolated singularity thus transcends its limits to revel in communal symbiosis.

In this context, herethics takes on new meanings. It is not merely the heretic's ethics, but is *her* ethics, the woman's ethics. It is the ethics of a woman who does not shut herself up in her singularity. The semiotic in her empowers her to shatter the narrow confines of the ego and embrace others with love. Her ethics helps her be in communion with her community, which proves to be the first step in the process of subjectification.

Gender issues that necessitate an alternative ethics, a her-ethics, are universal because traditional cultures relegate women to a pre-cultural, pre-discursive position. But certain issues are, obviously, context-specific. In the Indian context, especially in the brahminical society of Bengal, it was the unethical observance of brahminical dharma that problematised the upper caste women's lives. The disparity in the ideology and practice of *dharma* alerts us to the dynamics of gender in the brahminical society.

The 'woman question' in the socio-cultural context of Bengal demands a serious enquiry because Bengal claims to be different from the other states of India in many respects. The cultural and demographic profiles of Bengal project forth certain progressive features and liberal norms. Land of reformers, spiritual leaders and educationists, the state has rightful claims about the ideologies that made it flag-bearer of reform. But behind the sun-lit, open spaces, there were dark patches of ignominious customs. Life was not very progressive in the brahminical society of Bengal even at the turn of the twentieth century.

The disparity in the ideology and practice of *dharma* alert us to the dynamics of gender in the brahminical society. *Dharma*, the ancient equivalent of normative ethics, was the central informing power of the brahmin's life. Julia Leslie explicates the term *dharma* thus:

> In its widest, cosmic sense, *dharma* is the law of the universe, the fundamental order sustaining the world, inherent in the very nature of things. Both descriptive and prescriptive, it indicates both what is and what ought to be, the real and the ideal. In the realm of individual action, therefore it embraces

> both what one does and what one ought to do. Each individual's action defined by birth and circumstances, is his duty, it was ordained to be so and is therefore right. (*The Perfect Wife* 263)

The social positions, duties and privileges of the members of the four *varnas*, castes, were explicitly stated in the *Vedas* and the *Smritis* or the sacred law books. The stipulations regarding the duties and the privileges of the brahmin are laid down in great detail in *Manu Smriti* but there were incredible differences between the ideal and the real in the conceptualization and practice of *dharma* in the male world.

The ethical practice is most acutely problematised by the discrepancy between the ideal and the real in relation with man's duty towards woman. Indifference to the rules which were meant to correct and guide the male was common. But the patriarchal attitude to those which defined and regulated man-woman relationship was one of studied indifference and more poignantly, active rejection. The callousness of the system and the clever manipulations become all the more pronounced when we see the societal attitude of pushing the *slokas* which uphold the rights of women to the periphery while bringing the *slokas* where Manu exhort a wife to worship her husband as a veritable god to the forefront. In the ideal context both the rights and the duties were inter related. But the directives related to the first were conveniently forgotten while those concerned with the second were widely quoted and instilled in to the psyche of the collective.

In the case of the female, the ideal and the real were expected to be the same. The prescriptions of law were to be followed to the letter. According to Manu "A wife should always present a smiling face, should be alert and clever in her domestic duties, should keep vessels well burnished and clean and should not be extravagant." (*Manusmriti* V, 150). He adds that the habit of drinking wine, keeping company of bad people, staying away from husband, wandering about (on pilgrimages or elsewhere), sleeping by day and staying in the house of strangers were the six vices that spoilt women. (IX, 13). The *Skanda Purana* defines the *pativrata* as someone who does not cry loudly even when she is publicly blamed and one who keeps on smiling even when she is beaten (qtd. Kane, *History of Dharmashastra* 565). For a very long time, the picture of the *pativrata* had a strong hold over the male imagination and made the brahmin woman's life miserable. Kane quotes the sage Sankha who was most explicit about the decent conduct of a wife:

> She should not go out of the house unless she is asked [by her husband or elders] nor without putting an upper garment; she should not walk fast; she should not speak with a male who is unrelated to her (except a trader, a *sanyasin,* an old man or a physician); she should not allow her navel to be seen; she should wear her garment in such a way that it may reach down to her ankles; she should not expose her breasts; she should not laugh loudly without covering her mouth (with her hand or her garment); she should not hate her husband or relatives; she should not be in the company of dancing girls, gambling women, women who make assignments to meet lovers, female ascetics, female fortune-tellers, women who live by tricks, magical and secret rites and who are of bad character; since (the wise declare that) the character of the women of good family is spoilt by bad company. (*History of Dharmashastra* 564)

Curiously enough, the male never allowed any relaxation in the practice of such rules. These prescriptions of Manu and Sankha restrained a woman in three ways. It curtailed her freedom of speech and her freedom of travel. It took away her right to dress as she wished. And most significantly it prevented her from mingling with the others of her community under the guise of protecting her from bad company. The oft-quoted dictum of Manu which proclaimed that woman was not to do anything independently put the final seal on the brahmin female's freedom.

Down the centuries the male world has been consistently and vociferously arguing that the censures against women were part of a protectionist ideology. P.V Kane says: "The object therefore of the authors that censured women was to inculcate the great value of chastity and obedience for women and not merely to paint a dark picture of them." (581). But a deeper probe brings out the badly hidden strategy behind the protectionist ideology. Behind the censure was a deep-seated suspicion of female volition and still behind it was the fear of female sexuality. As Jasodhara Bagchi says:

> The community's control over female sexuality lies at the centre of patriarchy. Female sexuality is as much loaded with the semiosis of woman's social existence as by her private familial one. The semiotic load, taking the garb of culture, called upon to contain the so-called 'natural', 'biological', 'overflowing', 'turbulent' female sexuality, was one of the chief markers of 'class' boundary of respectability. (*Embodiment* 78)

Concern for class/caste purity made the patriarchal brahminical society tighten the fetters around women and at every step in their lives, the cruel iron cut into their very spirit.

The dualism of brahminical dharma continued to problematise the life of the brahmin women even in the twentieth century. The brahmin male remained oblivious to the need for change in matters of law and ethics because he had the prerogatives of both the real and the ideal. Thus life in the brahminical society remained stagnant and stagnation made it corrupt. The males were blind to the changes that were occurring in the world around them and clung onto the orthodox, obsolete beliefs. The gendered dichotomy, in all the multifarious levels of life, threw in to sharp relief the pretensions of the paternalist self-image of the brahmin. He professed that he was the embodiment of *dharma*, but his actions proved otherwise.

Ashapurna Devi and Sulekha Sanyal draw upon this constitutive cultural and historical moment. They alert us to the silence that surrounded the life of women in the upper castes and make their transgressions, even though rare and far-spaced, the subject of literary enquiry and documentation. They identify the potential subjects and trace their attempts to actualize their potential. But they are not content with laudatory accounts of the singular woman who transcends to personhood and so trace the semiotic present in the psyche of the strong woman and narrate how the presence of the semiotic enables her to bond with her collective. Most importantly, they extend their enquiry into the role of women in social changes and thus interrogate the absolutism of male-oriented history.

Chapter II

Negotiations in Patriarchal Spaces

Pratham Pratisruti, Subarnalatha, Bakulkatha, and *Nabankur* are situated in a social milieu in which sexual differences are organised in codes that structure everyday life. The central informing power behind these codes is patriarchy and thus they become explorations into patriarchal hierarchies. As the individual family unit is at the core of patriarchy, these narratives move deductively from the familial to the social milieu.

Masculine assumptions had succeeded in moulding the entire gamut of political, social and familial structures in the brahmins' world and the power of the male permeated everything. Speaking about patriarchal societies, Adrienne Rich says:

> Patriarchy is the power of the fathers: a familial-social, ideological, political system in which men—by force, direct pressure, or through ritual, tradition, law and language, customs, etiquette, education, and the division of labour, determine what part women shall or shall not play, and in which the female is everywhere subsumed under the male. (*Of Woman Born* 57).

This observation is very true in the case of brahminical system of life.

In the trilogy and in *Nabankur* the mutually exclusive male and female spaces in the brahmin household are well marked and the different characters are situated in the various strata of power. The negotiations that take place in the three spaces, the anterior space of the males, the negotiating space of the elder women and the posterior space of the younger women, for and against female transcendence to personhood form part of the core of the theme.

In the male space, power is the primal word, but there are subtle currents that make some more powerful than the others. Power is defined by the different, self-assigned roles a man takes up. They may rightly be called agents, accomplices and compliers according to the power they wield in the family and society. The aggressive agent of the brahminical law at the apex is the most powerful. Below him there are the active accomplices and the passive compliers (the roles overlap very often), who bask in reflected glory and whose only strength lies in the sanctions provided by the society. A crucial truth that surfaces is the male world's indifference, and sometimes even active hostility, towards female subjectification. The lords of the male space in the novels, irrespective of age, education, and chances of exposure to the modern ways of life, adamantly cling on to their conviction that woman has no right to personhood.

In the negotiating space the elder women are averse to the younger women's attempts to become subjects. But later, at least some of them are influenced by their daughters and granddaughters and develop a changed female perspective. The rising female consciousness succeeds in making its imprint, though unwelcome most often, here also.

In the posterior space, there are four categories of women. At the highest stratum of awakening: there are those who strive to actualize their dormant potential, and at the lowest, there are the completely unawakened ones. In between, there are two intermediate positions; in the first, there are women who are vaguely aware of their urges, but do not attempt to realize them, and in the second are those, even though they lack the potential to grow into subjecthood, who offer moral support to the potential subjects.

In their narratives, Ashapurna Devi and Sulekha Sanyal identify various forms of conceptually embedded gender biases and portray a multi-layered power structure. Ramkali Chatterjee in *Pratham Pratishruti* and Dakshinaranjan Ray in *Nabankur* are the agents of brahminical power. They are the agents of the codes of law because caste, wealth and familial and social positions conspire to invest in them the right to interpret law as they choose. They follow it to the very letter if they so wish, or remain totally indifferent to it. There are times when they actively reject it altogether. But their power is so absolute that they are never challenged.

The men of the second generation, Nabakumar in *PrathamPratishruti* and Prabodhchandran in *Subarnalatha* are accomplices. The men of the third generation, the sons of Satyabati in *Pratham Pratishruti* and Subarna in *Subarnalatha*, are, generally, passive compliers. The narratives project the fact that the changes initiated by factors like modern education and urbanization can be peripheral if true sympathy is absent.

Ramkali Chatterjee, in *Pratham Pratishruti*, is an unusual brahmin, a rebel against brahminical practices in his own way and a series of transgressions mark him as different from the greedy, lazy, ignorant brahmins around him. He holds the village spellbound with his majestic good looks, great wealth and unlimited generosity. He is so awe-inspiring that even the toughest, most orthodox brahmins fear to challenge him. He braves the anger and condemnation of his society with his unflinching moral standards many a time and succeeds to get his own way. But Ramkali never uses his forceful personality to set right the evil practices of the society, which directly affect the female world around him. Jasodhara Bagchi observes, "He remained straight as a ramrod in performing what he considered to be his duty, but this did not prevent him from being an unflinching patriarch." (Foreword to *The First Promise* X)

Three constitutive elements in Ramkali's psyche mark him as a symbol of patriarchy: his faith in the superiority of rationality over emotionality, his active involvement in the perpetuation of certain forms of patriarchy and his attitude to the widows in his family. Ramkali is educated and cultured and so ostentatiously respects women, but deep within him, there is only contempt for the quarrelsome, 'ignorant, talkative frailty' called women. To him "women as a race were narrow minded and orthodox. Of course they were called the goddesses of the hearth, out of courtesy nothing else. In reality, they were the incarnations of misery." (*First Promise* 72) This contempt is rooted in the belief that women are emotional and hence inferior beings. He is intolerant of emotional outbursts of all kinds irrespective of the cause, the context and the person involved. He fails to understand the pain of Sarada, his nephew's wife, when a co-wife is thrust upon her, and ignores the silent tears of his wife Bhuvaneswari when their only child is sent away to her very distant affinal home. Adrienne Rich's description of the patriarch and his power suits Ramkali Chatterjee very well.

The powerful person would seem to have a good deal at stake in suppressing or denying his awareness of the personal reality of others; power seems to engender a kind of willed ignorance, a moral stupidity, about the inwardness of others, hence of oneself. This quality has been variously described as "detachment", "objectivity", "sanity"—as if the recognition of another's being would open the floodgates to panic and hysteria. (*Of Woman Born* 65)

In Ramkali's world, essentially a male world, genuine knowledge of the other is unnecessary and so he interprets the language of silence and tears as jealousy and possessiveness and dismisses them as unworthy of consideration. It is this cold detachment that makes his perspicacious daughter, Satya, ask him: "As a doctor you read symptoms from a patient's appearance and you know exactly what is happening inside his body, Baba, don't you? So can't you guess what is going on inside a person by looking at the face?" (*First Promise* 73)

In matters of inheritance Ramkali Chatterjee adheres strictly to the *Dharmashastras*. Chatterjee approves of the birth right of the male and so, even though most of his great wealth is his personal acquisition, he vehemently opposes the very idea of his daughter inheriting it and declares the boys in the family as the rightful heirs to it. The small piece of land offered to Satya is far away from the village, at Triveni, and effectively uproots her from not only her natal family but even from her village. Thus the self-made Ramkali becomes instrumental in creating one more generation of lazy brahmins who live off the land without ever having to prove their personal worth.

Ramkali Chatterjee's attitude to the widows further reaffirms his unflinching patriarchal stance. He remains completely ignorant of the plight of the widows in his own household and believes that sacrifice is their lot in life and should be accepted without grumbling. Ashapurna Devi foregrounds the blatant double standards of patriarchal interpretation of law through Ramkali here. He adheres to the law when it is favourable to the male and ignores it when it is favourable to the female. This scholarly brahmin who insists on clarifying his spiritual and moral doubts with the help of his *guru*, never feels it necessary to subject him to a self-interrogation regarding the correctness of his stand about the widows. He remains completely indifferent to the *smritis* that stipulate five situations in which a woman is allowed to remarry and never makes any compromise with his staunch belief that a widow should lead a life of sacrifice. When Shankari, a young widow disappears from the antahpuram, his moral dilemma is rooted in the inner conflict between his *dharma* as a righteous individual and his concern for his family's honour and the question that torments him is whether to divulge it or not. In the patriarchal value system, concepts like man's pride and family's honour are directly related to the female's chastity and in the midst of these loudly asserted notions, the young widow's silent pleas pale into insignificance. Ramkali's attitude does not change over the years and so when Satya plans to get Sankari's daughter, Suhasini, married, he is resistant to the idea. To him Suhasini's birth itself is a mistake and hence she will propagate only a defective family. He disinclines to look into the role of the man in generating mistakes.

Ramkali lives in a socio-cultural milieu where the ethical practice is most acutely problematised by the discrepancy between the ideal and the real in relation with man's duty towards woman. Ironically, this noble brahmin, who is hailed as the very embodiment of ethics and moral uprightness is completely unconscious of the discrepancy. An analysis of Ramkali Chatterjee's attitudinal fluctuations reveals that to the patriarch, *dharma* means more the convenience of the powerful than an all-embracing justice. He is not unduly concerned about the impact of his decisions in the female space of his family even if the decisions directly affect those closest to him. When he conducts *gauridaana*, which means giving an eight-year-old girl child away in marriage, he is in fact rejecting the *Manusmriti*, the most authentic text of law for the brahmins. Manu categorically states that there is nothing wrong in a girl remaining unmarried, even to the end of her life, if a suitable bridegroom is not found (*Manusmriti* IX 89). Obviously the sage had not completely neglected the importance of compatibility between the bride and the bridegroom as an important factor of a successful marriage and expects the parents to exercise caution in choosing the bridegroom for their little daughter. But to the brahmin patriarchs, a post puberty unmarried girl was a curse and a disgrace to the family. Thus the question of mental, physical and intellectual compatibility was never raised. Ramkali follows the tradition and gives his little daughter in marriage without making sufficient enquiries about the bridegroom and his family. It is an error which has far-reaching consequences that affect the female genealogy of his family for three generations.

The same patriarchal perceptions and priorities characterise the male spaces in *Nabankur* also and the men who reign there are incredibly similar to one another in spite of individual differences.

Sulekha Sanyal, in *Nabankur*, portrays the most detestable form of the patriarchal power structure because here, money, caste and gender are equal players in the politics of power. The female protagonist's grandfather Dakshinaranjan Ray's Bengal is almost half a century away from Ramkali Chatterjee's and so he lives in a world made complex by politics, war, famine, recession and above all by an awakening consciousness among the marginalized categories in society. But the basic features that symbolize them as patriarchal males continue to be the same. Discussing the psychodynamics of masculinity and the repression of affective relational needs, Chodorow says: "men tend to repress their oedipal needs for love and relationship. At the same time, men often become intolerant and disparaging of those who can express needs for love, as they attempt to deny their own needs." (*The Psychodynamics of the Family* 185) This observation is true in the case of both Ramkali Chatterjee and Dakshinaranjan Ray.

Money and power are terms Dakshinaranjan Ray well understands, but patriotism and political ideologies are not. But what irritates him most, more than political and social changes, more than the innumerable legal battles that impoverish him, is the attempt of his granddaughter to individuate. As Chhobi's brother rightly puts it, he cannot stand Chhobi. His dislike is rooted in Chhobi's negation of the traditional mould of the good brahmin girl who is obedient, docile and hard-working. He considers this defiant daughter of the family, who roams in the village like a peasant girl, who is politically alert and has a socialistic turn of mind, as the bane of an upper caste, aristocratic family. Like all autocrats, his ego cannot accept any one else in his family, especially a woman, to be a part of the decision-making process. He is used to a system where man decides and woman obeys. Even in his death bed, Ray cannot tolerate the mention of Chhobi's name. All the pent-up anger and frustration pours out when his wife informs him of the birth of another granddaughter. "'Girl?' His face twisted in a grimace and he closed his eyes again. Then he slowly said 'Kill her!'" (*Nabankur* 233)

But this same brahmin, who is proud of his noble lineage, can stoop to very low level when he chooses. Like Ramkali Chatterjee of *Pratham Pratishruti*, he ignores tradition when it suits him. When the family's fortunes deteriorate, he very conveniently forgets the *shastra* that a brahmin should acquire wealth only just sufficient to maintain himself and his family, and to enable him to perform his religious duties without causing any harm to others or by as little harm to others as possible. During the Bengal famine, he instigates his son to enter into black marketeering. The anguish of the hundreds who starve does not touch his stony heart. Thus Dakshinaranjan is callously indifferent to male brahminical *dharma* but, at the same time, he will not allow the females of his household to make even a minor transgression.

The male space is not a homogenous entity. Ashapurna Devi and Sulekha Sanyal are aware of the subtle shifts in power that created different layers in the patriarchal society. Their novels depict the multifarious male world to perfection. Only strong willed men like Ramkali Chatterjee and Dakshinaranjan Ray can be active agents in the power structure of the brahmin society. The majority in the male world are accomplices who extend unconditional support to the agents and bask in the power conferred on them by the more powerful men.

Nabakumar in *Pratham Pratishruti* is an accomplice of patriarchy all through his life. With incisive understanding, Ramkali assesses his son-in-law thus. "A pleasant face, not an intelligent one though. He smiled regretfully to himself. It was possible to be fond of him, but one could hardly depend on him." (*First Promise* 295) The weak, ineffectual Nabakumar loves his wife, Satyabati, but wistfully wonders how different life would have been if only she were a doll-like—beautiful, smiling but silent—wife. He quails before his wife's courage when she stands up against his mother and whenever possible runs away from unpleasant situations.

Unlike the powerful males in the novels already mentioned, Nabakumar is a coward and like the primordial male backs out of sharing the blame even as he enjoys the pleasures and comforts of life which are hard won by the struggles of Satya. Whenever Satya takes a step in the direction of her dream of creating a world where men and women can live as dignified human beings, he tries to stop her saying, "What my mother says is true. A woman's learning is the origin of all destruction." (317). But in the absence of a powerful agent, the weak-willed accomplice cannot impose his will on his wife. So he uses harsh words when angry and grovels when he gets over it. The orthodox male in him shouts and raves every time when she tries to assert her independence—

when she tries to take up the responsibility of bringing up Suhasini, Shankari's orphaned daughter; when she starts learning English; when she starts teaching in the Sarvamangala Vidyalaya; when she insists on her sons completing their education before they start earning—but he instinctively knows that she has grown beyond his reach.

Men like Nabakumar need an excuse to hide behind and to get their thoughtless actions endorsed and in most cases it is *matru bhakti*, the devotion to the mother, which functions as their shield. One is forced to be cautious about the sincerity of their sentiments because the two constitutive elements of *matru bhakti*, the faith in the greatness of the mother and the fear of her curse, can be clever tools in the hands of a male.

When a man causes irredeemable misery to his wife and daughter and puts the blame on his mother, he is actually doing an injustice to all the three women concerned. Nabakumar breaks his promise to Satya and gives his eight-year-old daughter in marriage without her consent and in her absence. He brazenly tries to appease Satya by saying that he was cornered by his mother and when he fails, he tries to justify himself on the ground that her own father had made *gauridaana* when she was eight. Thus like a true patriarchal accomplice he follows the practice of the powerful even though he lacks the courage to face the consequences.

Nabakumar is only an accomplice in a crime perpetuated by the society but his sin is more unforgivable than that of the older generation. He is educated, has seen the world changing and above all he has a wife who is a child of light if only he had the eyes to see. He is guilt-stricken but instead of admitting guilt, he resorts to anger. When Satya renounces the family and leaves for Benaras, he rages and curses her: "It is not good for a woman to be so daring. I tell you you'll have a real hard time. That's my curse, as your husband." (532)

Prabodh Chandran, Subarna's husband, in *Subarnalatha* is another prominent accomplice of patriarchal law and proves that changing times have failed to make any positive change in the male consciousness. He is an average male of his time. His world is one of basic instincts. The men of his world move around the primordial urges of hunger, hegemonic power relations and sex. Anyone who is different is branded and ridiculed as mad.

He obeys the patriarchal norms by worshipping his mother and humiliating his wife, by refusing to educate his daughters and above all by treating his wife as a body without a mind. Her healthy body drives him mad with desire but her open, innocent mind pushes him into sexual jealousy. Thus he tortures and humiliates Subarna, accusing her of having illicit relationship with men like Mallik babu who supplies Subarna with books and Ambika Kumar, the freedom fighter. He does not know that they are the metaphorical windows which enable Subarna to look out from her prison at the outside world of freedom. In his perspective, man-woman relationship has only one dimension, the sexual. In the first phase of the battle of the two wills, Prabodh's and Subarna's, Prabodh is supported by his mother and brothers and in the last phase by his sons. Thus the patriarchal agenda of keeping the woman subjugated is reaffirmed.

The men of the third generation, Satyabati's sons in *Pratham Pratishruti* and Subarna's sons in *Subarnalatha* belong to the lowest stratum of power because they are the passive compliers. They are yet to achieve the agency to create or interpret the codes of law and hence are not directly involved in the oppression of the females in the family. Yet they are potential oppressors because they reject the mother to enter the kingdom of the father. The critical enquiries of feminist thinkers and mothering theorists into the psychodynamics of rejection reveal the basic difference in the male and female subject formation.

Julia Kristeva, the French feminist critic, has developed a notion of abjection which is very useful in diagnosing the dynamics of oppression: "Matricide is our vital necessity, the sine-qua-non of our individuation" (*Black Sun* 27). Both sexes must give up the mother to develop an exogamous libidinal relation and speaking position independent of her. The child grows away from the semiotic chora, the preverbal space preceding meaning and signification where he is completely dependent on the mother. The semiotic motility is transferred to symbolic order. But this sacrifice and separation is most intense and acute in the case of the son. He develops an introjected identification with the father's authority and rejects the mother.

The fear, which leads to the rejection of the mother, is a recurrent motif in many myths. In *Of Woman Born*, Rich quotes Frieda Fromme-Reichmann who narrates a Persian myth to bring out the dynamics of rejection and oppression:

> there is a Persian myth of the creation of the World which precedes the biblical one. In that myth a woman creates the world, and she creates it by the act of natural creativity which is hers and which cannot be duplicated by men. She gives birth to a great number of sons. The sons, greatly puzzled by this act which they cannot duplicate, become frightened. They think, 'Who can tell us, that if she can *give* life, she cannot also *take* life.' And so, because of their fear of this mysterious ability of woman, and of its reversible possibility, they kill her. (110)

Kristeva also observes: "The fear of the archaic mother turns out to be essentially fear of her generative power. It is this power, a dreaded one, that patrilineal filiation has the burden of subduing" (*Powers of Horror* 77). Both writers argue that a sense of shame, rooted in the knowledge that he was once only a helpless clot of flesh growing inside her, combined with the fear of her generative power, compels the son to reject the mother.

The concept of rejection, discussed by Adrienne Rich in nineteen seventy six and developed into the psycho-analytical theory of abjection by Julia Kristeva in nineteen eighty-two, had already been documented and debated by Ashapurna Devi in the nineteen sixties. It foregrounds the enormous importance placed by women writers, belonging to different cultural and temporal contexts, on the difference in the subject formation patterns of boys and girls. Ashapurna Devi locates the reason for the abjection in the son's sense of inferiority. In the second novel in the trilogy, *Subarnalatha*, she observes that the son feels ashamed of having once sought refuge in the mother's body, for having been brought to this world and for having been brought up by her. He knows intuitively that it is a great debt that cannot be repaid in terms of money. The unpaid debt makes him ashamed and then angry and finally leads to the abjection of the mother. (212) It is crucially important that the matricidal drive is not as powerful in the daughter as it is in the son. Kristeva says:

> For a woman, whose spectacular identification with the mother as well as the introjection of the maternal body and self are more immediate, such an inversion of matricidal drive into a death-bearing maternal image is more difficult, if not impossible. Indeed how can She be that bloodthirsty Fury, since I am She (sexually and narcissistically), She is I? (*Black Sun* 28, 29)

The sons in *Pratham Pratishruti* and *Subarnalatha* are passive compliers and project the attitudinal differences of sons and daughters. Just as the father appreciates a docile daughter and the husband a docile wife, the sons approve of a gentle, sweet tempered mother who never breaks the domestic peace. If the mother turns out to be different, if she refuses to conform, they comply with the dictates of the patriarchal society without ever bothering to find out why their mother has become a resistante. It is interesting to study the son's attitude to a mother who subverts the conventional notions of motherhood in comparison with that of the daughter. Most women scholars and psychoanalysts who focus on the mother-daughter relationship believe that the daughter respects a mother who is capable of being different. In her seminal text, My *Mother/ My Self,* Nancy Friday vehemently argues that the daughter prefers a mother who tries to assert her identity to a mother who allows herself to be objectified. Solid, empirical evidence can be gathered from the accounts of two remarkable daughters in *Janani—Mothers, Daughters, Motherhood*, who discuss their relationship with their mothers--Bharati Ray and C.S. Lakshmi. Bharati Ray makes an introspection and admits that she could never appreciate her mother because her mother was an exceptionally gifted woman who invisibilised herself in a life choking with housework, never bothering to nurture her gifts. C.S. Lakshmi, on the other hand, is extremely proud of her mother, Alamelu, because she was a woman who obeyed her heart, whether it be to follow her dead husband to the cremation grounds and bid him farewell by singing a song he loved best, or to go to Chennai to learn a particular aspect of *Carnatic* music when she was in her late sixties. But the daughter's admiration for the mother who defies custom is not reflected in the son. He internalizes the traditional, patriarchal definitions of motherhood so thoroughly that he perceives his mother merely as a mother and never as an autonomous being. His autonomy is achieved by rejecting her.

Satyabati, in *Pratham Pratishruti*, is no stranger to the ways in which the male world would try to subjugate a woman. She has experienced their anger and sarcasm 'but the unkindest cut' comes from her sons. This wound is all the more painful because it is inflicted by her own flesh and blood.

Satya is urged on by a desire to save her sons, Sadhan and Saral, from a stale, decadent system. She wants them to grow up as dignified human beings. She manages to give them the best education possible, hoping that they will derive their sense of right and wrong through it. But they grow away from her and become her critics, especially Sadhan, the eldest son. He considers her sympathy for her community as a mental ailment. Over the years, Sadhan's sympathy for his father remains intact, but his sympathy for his mother diminishes. To him, Satya is always disrupting the peace of the family and insulting his father and feels that it is very unfair. At the very last moment, when she goes away forever, Sadhan is angry and irritated with her. "Sadhan had felt too annoyed with his mother to come along. His father might have done something unsanctioned, but the shameless commotion created by his mother was far worse, and unbearable." (*First Promise* 533) Sadhan, thus, is a true representative of a hegemonic system where man's sins are forgiven while woman's resistance is viewed with impatience. He also shows how slow the changes are in coming and how heartbreakingly blind one's own flesh and blood can be.

Saral, the second son of Satya and Nabakumar, is of a different mould. He tells his mother, "There are millions of wrongs in the world, just as there are millions of people. Your eyes will go blind, if you try to look at all of them. Isn't enough to see that you don't do wrong yourself?" (495). He is neither an accomplice nor a complier in the strict sense, but he will not take the trouble of righting the wrongs and will never interfere or express his opinions about the relative justice of his parents' actions.

In *Subarnalatha*, Subarna had hoped that her sons would understand her and that they would always be an inalienable part of her. But her sons never try to understand her. They cannot fathom her hopes and dreams. They see only her shrewish, battle crazy nature and fail to see that their cultured, dignified mother has lost all her sweetness because she has been forced to wage battle after battle. Her orthodox husband and his brothers had turned Subarna's conjugal home a cage and now her sons try to strengthen the bars of the cage. When Bhanu, her eldest son, begins to articulate each letter of the word 'woman', not mother or sister, with infinite sarcasm, she recognizes the painful reality that her sons are not different from the men of the previous generations. These men of the third generation thus foreground the crucial truth that education and urbanization cannot hope to have much impact when sentience is completely absent. There are others like Pradeep, Chhobi's brother in *Nabankur*, and Subal, Subarna's youngest son in *Subarnalatha*, who do not approve of the absolutism of patriarchal power, but they will not help their mothers or sisters because they are masters of evasion.

These are the lords and masters of the male, public spheres. Their all-pervading power keeps the female sphere under their sway and creates innumerable difficulties in the path of the woman in her journey to personhood.

Between the male and female spaces of the brahmins' household there is a negotiating space, occupied by the elder women who are entrusted with the power to rule the antahpuram. These elder women mediate with the male world, internalize its potentially oppressive prescriptions and implement them in the female world. Exploring the space of the mother in the 'Kingdom of the Fathers', Adrienne Rich observes: "Patriarchy depends on the mother to act as a conservative influence, imprinting future adults with patriarchal values." (*Of Woman Born* 61)

Sexism is perpetrated not only by the oppressors but by the oppressed themselves who are socialized in such a way that they act in complicity with the oppressor. Gloria Watkins observes: "Between women, male supremacist values are expressed through suspicious, defensive, competitive behaviour. It is sexism that leads women to feel threatened by one another without cause." (*Feminist Theory* 48) Patriarchy never allows any bonding to be forged among women. Women are kept confined to their multilayered spaces and are never given chances to develop a dialogic relationship. The feeling of oneness, a sense of belonging to the same community and a need and urge for bonding will naturally lead to empowerment which in its turn will enable women to question the dictates of patriarchy. So deliberate attempts are made to create and maintain chasms within the female world. Individual voices are forced to remain lone.

One of the surest and meanest weapons used by patriarchy against resistance is the mother-in-law or the elder woman. She is used to curb the spirit and volition of the younger women. In an interview with Anima Bose, Ashapurna Devi elucidates the strange workings of the mind of the elder women who make the lives of the younger women miserable: "Because they have, do and live with so little—they do not hesitate to hurt for very little; because they are deprived, they attack hungrily." (*The Book Review* 19.9) Transferred resentments sour relationships which should have been marked with mutual understanding and sympathy. The pain suffered by one generation hardens into intolerance and the next generation is penalized for mistakes it has not committed.

Elokeshi, Satya's mother-in-law in *Pratham Pratishruti,* is an unlettered, narrow-minded woman, and from the beginning treats Satya as an adversary because of the differences in their perceptions. It is interesting to analyse the dynamics of loathing that makes a middle-aged woman place herself in an antagonistic position against an innocent child. Elokeshi's dislike of Satya is rooted in her own insecurities. Her society defines her as a wife and as a mother and her familial and societal status is determined by it. As in the case of the other women of her community, the respect she receives is solely due to her position as a married woman and as the mother of a son. Elokeshi is habituated to her society's prescriptions and practices and fails to think of herself as an autonomous human being and hence feels threatened by anything that intervenes between herself and the men in her life. The unspoken, badly hidden truth about her husband's moral lapses must be a source of terrible anguish to her. The spirited young bride, who refuses to be subsumed under her authority, further threatens her with the possibility of alienation from her son also. So Elokeshi fails to appreciate the dignity and generosity of the bride and misinterprets Satya's thoughts, words and actions as defiance against the family.

Relationships which are problematised by complete lack of awareness can be seen in *Subarnalatha* also. Muktakeshi, Subarna's mother-in-law in *Subarnalatha*, considers Subarna as a terrible misfortune that has fallen on her and complains that her household will burn down in the flames of Subarna's defiance. But if only she had looked in to her own mind, she would have seen that the flames within are more destructive and unbearable than Subarna's.

The power structure of the family remains unshakable and Muktakeshi feels safe till Subarna enters her household as a bride. Her sons are all devotees of the mother and the eldest daughter-in-law is as lifeless as a clay pot. But Subarna is full of life and laughter. She tries to usher in the winds of change and thus invites Muktakeshi's wrath. Curiously, their battle makes Subarna as tough as Muktakeshi herself (but without her meanness) and paves the way for a strange empathy. Women of the younger generations like Satyabati and Subarna are educated and awakened enough to let the past go. They, unlike the women of the older generation, do not introject the symbols of oppression. Nancy Friday observes: "Our job as adults is to understand the past, learn its lessons, and then let it go. Blaming mother is just a negative way of clinging to her still." (*My Mother/ Myself* 84). It is this awareness that makes the women of the younger generation different from the women of the older generation.

Purnasashi, Chhobi's grandmother in *Nabankur*, is a simultaneous source of fear for the daughters-in-law and grand-daughters and sweetness for the sons and grandsons. Only Chhobi dares to question her grandmother's gender bias. Both the grandmother and the child are unaware of their status and position as women, but in two entirely different ways. The grandmother is unaware of the fact that as human beings, women too have rights. She believes that ultimately a woman's only future lies in marriage and that her duty is to do unending domestic work without any complaints. Whenever Chhobi tries to assert her will, Purnasashi, blames it on education. Chhobi is also supremely unconscious of her marginal status as a girl in the patriarchal system and flatly refuses to accept that there is any difference between the boys in the family and girls like her.

Purnasashi is a representative of the women of the earlier generations who internalize and naturalize patriarchal prejudices. Her indifference to the anguish of the members of her own community is worth probing. Like Muktakeshi of *Subarnalatha*, she has repressed excruciatingly painful memories of mental and physical torture deep within her. The cruel past warps the very perceptions of the girl and when she grows up she fails to see that a woman is a person and that she deserves love and respect.

Elokeshi, Muktakeshi, and Purnasashi are powerful weapons in the hands of patriarchy. They are used to cut any sprouts of individuation and stunt the growth of the younger women. Their task is to see that there are no chances for the growth of a sisterhood, a companionship within the inner space and that the lives of the younger women remain fragmented. They are there to ensure that more and more Elokeshis and Muktakeshis are created out of the younger generations because patriarchy needs Elokeshis and Muktakeshis not Satyas, Subarnas, or Chhobis.

After the anterior male space and the negotiating space of the elder women, there is the posterior space of the younger women. The windows of the fictional world of Ashapurna Devi and Sulekha Sanyal open inward to let light and air in to the closed women's quarters of the brahmins' household. But the community of women there is not Kristeva's 'community of dolphins' because jouissance is an unknown quality and an impossibility there. Women of different ages, experiences and attitudes, from the child brides to the hapless widows, exist in the inner spaces. They are inheritors of several generations of unvoiced, unchronicled experiences. With infinite love and compassion, these two writers bring the *asuryam pasya* forward for all the world to see. The compelling women characters of their novels defy the conventional moulds. They are the representatives of the victimized womanhood with whom generations of women, across time, culture and language, could empathise.

The females in these novels, the inmates of the antahpuram, irrespective of their age and status, are scarred by their experiences at the hands of an insensitive society. But like the male community, the female community is also not a homogenized mass. All the inmates of the pantheon of misery are not mute victims. Among them there are women who are situated in the various stages of awakening.

The four protagonists in the four novels analysed here, Satyabati in *Pratham Pratishruti*, Subarna in *Subarnalatha*, Bakul in *Bakul Katha*, and Chhobi in *Nabankur* are potential subjects. There are three distinguishing features that mark them as different from the other women of their time: their refusal to submit themselves to the psychological conditioning (both in the familial and social levels) which would lull their urge for personhood back to sleep, permeable ego boundaries and, most importantly, a unified sensibility. Their unified sensibility is a synthesis of feeling and thought, and this unique gift helps them develop perceptions, which are confluences of intelligence and experience. Unlike their fellow sufferers, they do not seek refuge in cursing fate, verbal abuses, or silent tears but correlate individual problems with that of the collective, recognize the patriarchal dualistic norms as the source of the stifling prescriptions, and think of the ways to correct the socio-cultural imbalances. The consequent, widening, perspectives intensify their urge for personhood.

The basic familial and social power structures that stifle the protagonists are the same but Satyabati, and Subarna, are child wives and therefore their problems are different from that of Bakul and Chhobi. Several factors conspire to make the lives of these young brides miserable. While some of these factors are individual-specific, many are common to all. The burden of the social and familial expectations, the pain of a total uprooting and the anxiety about growing roots in an alien, and very often, hostile atmosphere are shared by all. The absence of the female's autonomy over her own body and the torture forced sex can inflict on a young female body problematise matters further.

The problems in Satyabati's life stem mainly from the incompatibilities between her and her conjugal family. She is a moral being forced to live in a corrupt society. As the daughter of a very wealthy and very dignified brahmin she is not used to the uncultured ways of living in the affinal family. The moral lapses, greed, meanness, abusive language and incessant internal quarrels that pollute the atmosphere weigh heavily on her mind and she is infuriated by the cowardice of her husband who tries to run away from problems. But what Elaine Showalter describes as the 'accommodating postures of femininity' are alien to her nature. Thus the nine-year-old child unwittingly becomes the arch enemy of Elokeshi, her-mother-in-law and lives in a system where she is completely bereft of love or support.

In Satya's case, the isolation is almost complete because of the great distance between her natal and conjugal villages. Added to this physical distance is the emotional distance caused by the unspoken resentment she feels against her noble, non-conformist father who has conformed to the socio-cultural prescriptions by conducting *gauridaana.* She has inherited his keen mind and his pride and has to individuate by growing away from him.

Elokeshi's resentment, Ramkali Chatterjee's emotional detachment and Nabakumar's cowardice are the three factors that make life an eternal struggle for Satya. But instead of choosing the familiar escape routes like fault-finding and quarrelling, Satya enters into an inner dialogue where she is both the interlocutor and the answerer. She is on a quest to find the true reason for female subjugation and locates it in ignorance. She refuses to believe the patriarchal myth that women are, by nature, inferior to men and is convinced that women's shortcomings should be attributed not to birth but to the absence of training and opportunities. Her status as the potential subject is reaffirmed by her passion for learning, which is not implanted by the male reformer. Tanika Sarkar's observations about Rasasundari Devi, the first Bengali woman to write an autobiography, whom she cites as the supreme symbol of the female urge for learning and personhood, suit Satya in this respect.

A pious Hindu housewife, spending her life in a non-reformed domestic environment where no woman ever learnt to read, was so driven by this sharp desire that she taught herself the letters in great secrecy and with difficulty. When she finally started reading, a measure of her triumph was conveyed by her coining of a magnificent new word to describe her own achievement and mastery over the word—*Jitakshara*. (*Hindu Wife, Hindu Nation* 48)

Satya, like Rasasundari Devi, becomes *Jitakshara*. She is not intimidated by the combined efforts of the family and the society to thwart her attempt to attain personhood and this fearlessness empowers her to row her boat out of the stagnant little pond of the present to the broad current of the future.

The second novel in Ashapurna Devi's trilogy, *Subarnalatha*, traces the life of Subarna, the protagonist, from childhood to middle age. Like her mother Satyabati, Subarna is displaced from a progressive to a rigidly orthodox family and is forced to live in an environment that refuses to understand her or offer her any support. She is the victim of a broken promise. Her father breaks the promise made to her mother, gives her away in marriage when she is only nine. The society of the *kulin* brahmins does not find any reason to castigate the man for breaking a promise, especially one made to a woman, while it castes out the woman who confronts him and defies conjugality as a sinner. It further decrees that the sins of the parents will visit the children and thus Subarna's life is stigmatized.

Subarna's poetic sensibility, idealism and intellectuality mark her as different from the others in the affinal family but difference, especially in a woman, is not appreciated by the society. She craves to live like a human being, to read, to be politically alert and to respond to the changing world outside. Her husband and his brothers cannot refrain from calling her mad because they cannot understand why people should ever bother about things other than eating, sleeping and gossiping. Their minds are as closed as the house they have built.

Subarna's problems are accentuated by her husband's attitude to love and sex. To Prabodh Chandran, love is physical and woman is an object of pleasure. But Subarna cannot be a mere body. She is a complete being in whom intellectuality and emotionality converge. Her jealous husband, ever hungry for her beautiful body, humiliates and abuses her in the presence of others during the day and caresses her body at night. This physical love where the heart is totally negated is Subarna's bane. Her womanhood is acknowledged only in the conjugal bed. Whenever she tries to resist it, she is branded as an unchaste woman to whom maintaining youth and beauty is more important than her duty towards her husband.

Thus the little girl lives in an atmosphere that is always stiflingly hot with criticism and castigation. The sarcasm, jealousy and meanness of this world are not at all conducive to the mental growth of a girl. But Subarna manages to transcend the huge barriers placed before her by keeping two forces in her psyche alive; the permeable ego boundaries that let her to be in communion with her collective and the creative sensibility that gives a vent to her anguish.

Bakul, Subarna's daughter and the protagonist of *Bakul Katha*, is different from her mother and grandmother in one respect. Her resistance is not as loud as theirs. She is brought up by a mother who defies the conventional notions of womanhood and motherhood and in an atmosphere where the battle of wills creates palpable tension. As a basically reticent person she finds refuge in silence.

Bakul, like Satya and Subarna before her, is ridiculed for her intellectual turn of mind. Her mental constitution is defined by a more pronounced intellectuality and in a family where female intellectuality has always been a dubious attribute she is a misfit. Her father and brothers deny her the chance for a formal education and then callously laughs at her lacks. They try to conceal their guilt for failing to find a suitable bridegroom for her in angry tirades against her independence. But Bakul's soft exterior hides an exceptionally steely determination that transforms her to a self-educated and self-reliant person. Her self-assigned role as the chronicler of life offers her a vantage point from where she observes life and thus, overtly, she is distant from the intense pressures to which her collective is subjected. But Bakul is a link in the genealogy of women who preach and practise herethics and her capacity to empathise with the oppressed equals that of her mother and grandmother. Her ties with her community are strong enough to make individual and collective transcendence a reality.

The four novels analysed in this study have the characteristics of the female bildungsroman and document the various stages of female subjecthood from nascence to fruition. At the beginning of the narratives, the protagonists are young girls. When the narrative opens in *Nabankur*, Chhobi, like Satya and Subarna, is a child of eight. But she lives in the early decades of the twentieth century and *gauridaana* has by now become an obsolete practice. Girls are allowed to attend the village school for one year before they get married at the age of twelve or thirteen. Thus, unlike Satya and Subarna, Chhobi is not married yet but this one difference in status does not save the little girl from patriarchal segregations and exploitations. Gender boundaries are inviolable in the Ray household and Chhobi is treated as a secondary citizen by her grandparents. She is too young to comprehend her supposed inferiority and thus becomes the object of their fury. The prejudice surfaces dramatically when Purnasashi refuses to serve her a second helping of food, which is a male prerogative and chastises her for being defiant.

The patriarchal and parochial system castigates Chhobi at every step of her life. Chhobi's admiration for her freedom fighter uncle, Adhir, is not leniently viewed by the family that remains consciously blind to the political upheavals around them. Her sympathy for the economically disadvantaged, low caste, villagers is interpreted as a challenge to class and caste propriety. Her notions about education and marriage are too modern and radical for their taste and hence reprehensible.

But nothing dissuades Chhobi from determinedly adhering to her decision to assert her individuality. Different experiences, emotional, intellectual and political are concretized into her coherent personality. She is incredibly similar to Satya in many ways. Like Satya, she has a superior intellect, which no boy in the family can match, an unflinching courage that trivializes personal anguish and a moral strength that inspires her to interrogate injustices of all kinds. Like Subarna, she is an idealist, is alert to the socio-political insurgences around and shares her infinite sympathy for the downtrodden. These faculties sustain her in her efforts to violate the imposing gender boundaries.

Next in the four-point scale of awareness, there are the women who are conscious of the vague stirrings of dissatisfaction. They interrogate the false sense of complacency within which a woman hides her anxieties and initiate a battle to win their rights. But unfortunately the qualities that characterize the potential subject are absent in them. They lack the sensibility that enables the subject to feel and think. Moreover miseries and failures make them loners and they reject the reciprocal, healing touch of the love of the community. Thus transcendence remains an unformed, disturbing idea, repressed deep within their psyche. Sarada and Shankari in *Pratham Pratishruti*, and Namita in *Bakul Katha* belong to this group.

In *Pratham Pratishruti*, Ashapurna Devi narrates the story of Sarada to illustrate how the brahmins refuse to interrogate their inhuman customs or to find out permanent solutions for the problems which corrupt the social fabric. Her story demonstrates how the patriarchal way of solving problems objectifies woman completely and trivializes her emotions. Ramkali Chatterjee, who is very conscious about his social and moral responsibilities, takes upon himself the task of saving his friend's daughter, Patli, from the terrible fate of becoming an unmarried widow. A brahmin of his social stature can at least initiate discussions about the fallacy of certain practices, but instead, he uses one error to set another right. He makes Rasbihari, his nephew, marry Patli and is supremely unaware of the pain he inflicts on Sarada, Rasbihari's first wife.

Sarada is very much in love with her husband Rasu and foolishly believes that love will be her talisman against the 'barb' of a co-wife. But then she realizes that in a patriarchal society, there are other, more important, matters like man's honour and the family's fair name than the promise made to a woman. The wound inflicted by the male eats into her very soul and she becomes a shell, an automaton that functions mechanically. Sarada is different from the ordinary women of her time because she believes that she is not a pawn to be shunted from one column to another, from the centre to the margin. She is keenly sensitive to the subtle shifts in the relationship between herself and her husband and is acutely aware of her rights as a wife. She is a proud woman with a forceful personality, but unlike the potential subjects already mentioned, she neither tries to interrogate the absolutism of male authority nor to situate her pain in the larger context of the community's. She does not actualize her dormant urge to become a complete being but becomes a loner and a cynic.

In the same novel, there is another woman who is painfully alive to the needs of her mind and body. Shankari is an eighteen-year-old widow and is incarcerated in the widow's world, which is one of never-ending winter. Colour, fragrance, dreams and laughter are deliberately, forcibly shut out of her life. Her beauty and youth prompt the champions of *dharma* to be suspicious of her moral strength and to tighten the fetters around her. The humiliating insinuations and complete lack of understanding tempt Shankari to escape and seek emotional refuge elsewhere. She does not reach the ideal world of love and security but becomes the heroine in a sad tale of seduction, betrayal and suicide. Ashapurna Devi brings out this particular widow from the matrix of marginality and gives language to her experiences because she is marked with a difference. Even though she does not complete the process of subjectification, the beginnings of a repudiation of patriarchal power can be seen in her.

Namita in *Bakul Katha*, the third novel in Ashapurna Devi's trilogy, is a rejected wife. The door of her husband's world is closed against her because it is a world of spirituality. Her husband renounces the material world to become a *sanyasin* and lives in *Rishikesh* and the young bride is left to the charity of his uncle. But Namita is deeply hurt by their charity symbolized in the form of food, shelter, good saris and ornaments. She is a proud woman and is aware of her rights as a wife and a human being. Repeated rejections push her first to the dark alleys of flesh trade, then to the glittering world of film industry and finally to suicide. As in the case of Shankari, Namita's story can also be read as the nascence of an identity that does not reach fruition.

Among the inmates of the antahpuram there is another category of women whose awareness about themselves is minimal and tangential. The absence of education and economic dependence problematise their lives further and so they are forced to make compromises. Thus they refrain from interrogating the male notion of female servility. But even though there is no active defiance in them, they are important in the scheme of female subjectification because they offer moral support to the potential subjects and encourage them to actualize their potential. Two characters, Saudamini in *Pratham Pratishruti*, and Durga in *Nabankur* can be identified as the sources of support for the subjects.

Saudamini (called Sadu), in *Pratham Pratishruti*, is a deserted wife. She is rejected because of her husband's insane sexual jealousy and welcomed back by the same man because of his unending lust. Thus Sadu, all through her life, is seen as a body and her life moves through a trajectory of rejection and subjection. She goes back to her husband, not because she has any foolish hopes about love, but because she wants to escape the status of an unwanted appendage in her uncle's family.

When Sadu's husband, by now a man well past middle age, turns his greedy, lustful gaze on her whom he had forsaken years ago, she remains silent. But an unspoken angry reproach flashes in her mind. "At this age, you look at the glow of my body instead of looking at my soul? Aren't you ashamed?" (442). But the anger and resentment remain mute because Sadu is bound in her condition of vassalage due to the lack of economic freedom.

Sadu is ignorant about the ways of the world and lacks the courage to demand what is rightfully her's from life. But this marginalized condition prompts her to look upto Satya, who symbolizes female power, with great admiration. Education and economic independence empower Satya to transgress, while in the absence of them, Sadu cannot hope for a qualitative change in her status. But unlike the average women of her time, the consciousness about her shortcomings does not make her hate the woman who triumphs over the same shortcomings. She remains, right from the beginning to the very end, the subject's most reliable and most perceptive friend.

Durga, a young widow in *Nabankur* represents suppressed anger, rebellion and desires but cannot break the chains and so remains an inmate of the closed interiors. Durga, Chhobi's classmate in the village school, is an ordinary brahmin girl who is completely unaware of her status and rights as a human being. The lesson that marriage is the ultimate objective of a girl's life is so deeply ingrained in the psyche of girls like Durga that they spend their time in school giggling and talking in hushed tones. Attitudinal differences keep Durga poles apart from Chhobi. Durga and the three other girls in their class are the products of a system that considers all signs of individuation as rebellion. Chhobi's hunger for education, her sentience and her budding political awareness are beyond them and so she is excluded from their group.

The unawakened, shrewish Durga gets married, as she had always hoped, but the marriage lasts only for ten months. Widowhood does not automatically put an end to a woman's love for life and her desires as the society expects it to. Durga is too young to accept her loss philosophically but does not know what to do about it. Her grief and discontent surface when she talks to Chhobi: "How long can I survive in this way? I was married for ten months only, out of which

I spent only ten days with my husband. Why did everything have to end so soon for me?" (*Nabankur* 164)

Durga lacks the innate gifts and training of Chhobi but at this dark phase of life, she recognizes the worth and importance of a resistante like Chhobi. She is hopeful that Chhobi will continue her studies and make something of her future. Then she will do something for victimized womanhood and help women like Durga find their way.

Durga subverts the male image of the widow by articulating her discontent and protest. Even though there is no active rebellion on her part, she is not ashamed to speak about her unfulfilled desires. Unlike Sarada she does not become a cynic and unlike Shankari and Namita she does not destroy herself. She confides in Chhobi about her anguish and her insufficiencies and it marks the beginning of a meaningful solidarity. Durga raises questions, even though she does not find answers. But raising questions itself is a mark of awakening.

The women who bring to fruition the promises latent in them form a very small minority in the posterior female space. Most women remain completely unaware of the absences in their lives. In the novels analysed here, there are many such characters. But one woman, Uma Sasi in *Subarnalatha*, is the most expressive example for a state of mind which is described as inauthenticity or bad faith by existentialists.

Uma Sasi, Muktakeshi's eldest daughter-in-law in *Subarnalatha*, is a timid woman, a 'clay pot', and believes that she is a nobody. She has no self-respect or confidence and trembles like a leaf when she witnesses Subarna's incredible audacity. Her refuge is the kitchen and when Subarna appoints a cook to cater to the needs of the large family, she weeps silently because she feels that she is now totally unwanted. Unlike Subarna, she cannot prove her worth by her mere presence.

Uma Sasi tries to please every one but does not win the love or respect of any one. In a system where only the toughest can survive, the silent, gentle Uma Sasi becomes a non-entity. She fails to make friendship with Subarna because she does not understand what drives Subarna on. She is denied the companionship of the other brides, Giribala and Bindu, because she is too naive and is ignorant of the subtleties of the games of power. Thus Uma Sasi lives on in the midst of change without knowing its significance. She will not create any difficulty for the potential subject, but will not extend a helping hand either. She considers herself to be part of an inert situation and cringes in fear when she meets a woman who tries to transcend it.

This is the polarized world of the brahmin household where the female is treated as an immanence and the male as a transcendence. A centripetal reading of the novels foregrounds the different strata of power in the apparently monolithic structure and reveals the psychodynamics of oppression, resistance and transcendence. In the male space, the response to female transcendence to personhood is almost uniformly negative, while the negotiating space records slightly divergent patterns and individual reactions. In the female space, there are a few women who attempt to actualize their dormant strengths and to crystallize their identity even though the large majority remains in ignorance and apathy.

Transcendence in this cultural milieu and hierarchical structure is not an easily achievable objective. The potential subject needs, along with the individual qualities that intensify her urge for autonomy, the support of her collective to transcend the barriers and to become a complete subject. The process of the actualization of *dynamis* thus is an individual and collective effort.

In this context, woman bonding becomes central to the narrative pattern of the novels analysed. Ashapurna Devi and Sulekha Sanyal analyse the psychodynamics of resistance and applaud the achiever-woman, but they are conscious about the crucial importance of woman bonding in defining the contours of individual and collective identity. They, therefore, employ their fiction to study the semiotics of woman-bonding and to trace its impact in the socio-cultural realm in which the novels are situated.

Chapter III

Configurations of Bonding

Patriarchal ideology had always been a critique of female relationships and had decreed them out of existence in literary texts. The clever politics of subsuming the relationship among women into the category of human relationships succeeded in dislodging woman bonding from the core position and making it remain, at best, as an insignificant subtext.

Women writers are now trying to prove that the story of relationships among women has been written even if it has not been read, that it constitutes the hidden subtext of many texts. Many of the stories in the mythologies of far-flung cultures can be read as tales of woman bonding. But as patriarchy has always been suspicious of, even scared of, the camaraderie of women, they were deliberately invisibilised as insignificant subtexts. Now they have gained in importance and have moved on from the position of the subtext to their rightful position as the crucial, core text. For example, the story of the Graie in Greek mythology has been treated merely as an incidental episode in Perseus' adventures, but now it is revisited to bring out the possibilities of a veiled significance. In her famous book, *The Communities of Women*, Nina Auerbach quotes them as the ultimate example for love among sisters. She says:

> The Graie are three mythical sisters who are isolated from time: Hesiod's *Theogeny* states baldly that they were born old. In the "now" of myth, they have a single eye between them,

> which is passed unfailingly from sister to sister. They spend their lives endowing each other with vision: apparently it has never occurred to any one sister to keep the eye and run away. That is the hero's job. Perseus steals the eye, forcing them to reveal the whereabouts of their other triad of sisters, the irresistibly hideous Gorgons. Once the Graie are dispossessed of their eye, the Gorgons are doomed. (*Communities of women* 3)

The myth foregrounds a sisterhood which is indelibly written into history by primordial human experience and speaks about the wise women for whom vision was never a jealously-kept personal possession. Their ever-open inner eye watched over the members of their collective, empowering them to face the challenges of a hostile world. But this core text had been decentred to bring the hero's exploits to the centre and the very possibility of woman bonding was vigorously contested. The Gorgons and the Graie continued to be remembered for their hideous looks, but the symbolic significance of the shared eye and the grayness was completely ignored.

But now, women writers all over the world repudiate the debilitating patriarchal strategy of trivializing female relationships. They are reconstructing textual strategies to produce an alternative discourse of woman bonding and empowerment. Contemporary studies are shifting their focus from examining women in relation to men to the emotional and social support of one woman for another, which is essential for each woman's transcendence to personhood. Women have learned to break the age-old silence by establishing dialogic relationships within their community and to challenge established norms through collective dialogue. This collective dialogue has become central to many studies in sociology, anthropology, psychoanalysis, literary theory and literature today.

It is crucially important that both the repressed messages in the timeless mythical stories and the critical enquiries of contemporary feminist scholarship reveal the linkage between woman bonding and authentic, female selfhood. Nancy Chodorow observes that feminine personality comes to be based less on repression of inner objects, and fixed and firm splits in the ego and more on retention and continuity of external relationships.

> From their Oedipus complex and its resolution, women's endo-psychic object-world becomes a more complex relational constellation than men's and women remain preoccupied with ongoing relational issues. Masculine personality, then, comes to be defined more in terms of denial of relation and connection (and denial of femininity), whereas feminine personality comes to include a fundamental definition of self in relationship. (*Reproduction of Mothering* 169)

This view is corroborated by Irene Claremont De Castillejo, a clinical psychologist who says, "the feminine is more nearly an attitude of acceptance, an awareness of the unity of all life and a readiness for relationship." (*Knowing Woman* 15)

Discussing the conceptual and theoretical sources of woman-bonding, Marianne Hirsch says, "There can be no systematic and theoretical study of women in patriarchal culture, there can be no theory of women's oppression, that does not take into account woman's role as a mother of daughters and as a daughter of mothers, that does not study female identity in relation to previous and subsequent generations of women." (*Mothers and Daughters* 202) Mother-daughter dyad thus becomes the basis on which the collectivity of women may be imagined and discoursed. This symbiotic relationship is relevant to woman-bonding and the resulting empowerment because it can affect the relational capacity of the daughter by making her ego boundaries permeable and also because the traces of the maternal enables her to enter the symbolic and to reconstruct it from within. Both feminist theoreticians and psychoanalysts recognize the quality of the pre-oedipal mother-daughter relationship as a transforming force, which can turn a woman's being from lonely singularity to a healthy plurality. As the psychodynamics of bonding among women is rooted in the cathexis between the mother and daughter, this study proposes first to analyze the mother-daughter dyads in the selected novels, and then to go on to kinship relations.

The mother-daughter bonding offers potentially crucial keys to the development of female consciousness. While discussing mother-daughter relationship in the context of the lives and works of Laura Ingalls Wilder and Rose Wilder Lane, Anita Clair Fellman observes that their own needs for nurturance and individuation informed the way they perceived the world. She substantiates her view by quoting Carol Gilligan, a psychoanalyst who says, "A sense of embeddedness based on the daughter's connectedness to her mother, characterizes women's ethical views." (*Laura Ingalls Wilder and Rose Wilder Lane* 540) But in spite of its centrality in women's lives, a strange silence used to surround it. Adrienne Rich argues that the reason for the absence of the mother-daughter relationship from theology, art, sociology and psychoanalysis lies in the male practice of relegating the female subjective experience to the margins. According to her, motherhood, as an institution in patriarchy, was shaped by male expectations and structures. The authority of female experience was trivialized and the objective rationality of the third person's voice—the male voice—interpreted motherhood, ignoring the strong emotional ties between the mother and daughter.

> The loss of the daughter to the mother, the mother to the daughter, is the essential female tragedy. We acknowledge

> Lear (father-daughter split), Hamlet (son and mother) and Oedipus (son and mother) as great embodiments of the human tragedy; but there is no presently enduring recognition of mother-daughter passion and rapture. (*Of Woman Born* 237)

Rich argues that there was a time when enormous importance was placed upon the mother-daughter dyad and quotes the Eleusinian Mysteries that celebrated the reunion of the mother and daughter as an example, even though the subsequent ages ignored it. Luce Irigaray also observes that the beginnings of patriarchal power coincided with the separation of daughters from mothers. She says:

> The mother-daughter relationship—the most fertile from the point of view of preserving life in peace—was destroyed to establish an order tied to private property, to the handing down of property within the male line of descent, to the institution of monogamous marriage so that property, including children, belong to this line of descent, and to the establishment of men-only social organisations for the same purpose. (*Thinking the Difference* 13, 14)

Now, there is a dramatic reversal of the silence and there are attempts to fill the voids created by silence and absence. In contemporary feminist studies and the various disciplines that intersect in it, the mother-daughter cathexis and the resultant relational capacities are widely discussed. Women writers now explore and define female identity focusing on relationship among women, especially the relationship between mother and daughter.

Thus Demeter and Persephone are reborn in many modern literary texts to speak about a beautiful aspect of human life, which has been repressed. For example, Angela Carter's *The Bloody Chamber* celebrates the assertion of the maternal power that can "undo rape and bring her [daughter] back from death". (*Of Woman Born* 240) The story is a domestication of the Demeter-Persephone myth. The potentially powerful mother-daughter love which defies destiny and death forms the core of the story while the Prince Charming, who saves the damsel in distress and the powerful father figure who protects the child from danger are conspicuously absent. The girl's description of her mother, who implements 'a furious justice' and rewrites her destiny, pulsates with love and awe: "On her eighteenth birthday, my mother had disposed of a man-eating tiger that had ravaged the villages in the hills north of Hanoi. Now, without a moment's hesitation, she raised my father's gun, took aim and put a single, irreproachable bullet through my husband's head." (*Bloody Chamber* 45) This narrative strategy of bringing powerful, autonomous females, who were pushed to the margins, back to the centre and analyzing them in the context of their community is a recurrent pattern now.

It is indeed gratifying to notice that the regional women writers of India had been aware of the significance of the seemingly contradictory concepts of autonomy and community even before the onset of active discussions worldwide and had placed their women characters in a dialectic of autonomy and community. The novels discussed in this study are celebrated as powerful bildungsromans, but the crucial importance placed on the relationship among women is generally ignored. Writers like Ashapurna Devi and Sulekha Sanyal are alert to the individual-collective dichotomy and are aware of the infinite possibilities of female communality, ideological activism and responsive creation of an alternative ethics. They assert that women's awareness of gender discrimination in the patriarchal culture and their awakening are inseparable from woman bonding. Their works, thus, become supreme expositions of what Julia Kristeva calls herethics.

While studying the reform movements in the twentieth century Kerala and the role of the woman and writer in it, J.

Devika quotes Lalithambika Antharjanam as the most powerful *Namboothiri* woman writer who portrays the Achiever Woman as a product of and part of the same sex collective. She observes that Antharjanam's works are powerful critiques of the individualization of gender: "The critique of the philosophy of the individual is a perennial theme in Antharjanam's work, more specifically, the ideal of the rational, competitive, self-sufficient, productive individual in the exclusive sense" (*Engendering Individuals* 235). She identifies certain important aspects in this critique. One aspect stresses the necessity of socialization while another highlights the independence and power of transcendence that the individual derives from social ties. Thus Antharjanam establishes the primacy of amicable, empowering relationships over lonely singularity. This observation is relevant to the work of Ashapurna Devi and Sulekha Sanyal also. The bonding forged among their female characters forbids the fracturing of identity and enacts a womanist subjectivity in which each woman is the agent and arbiter of her individual female destiny within the framework of her community.

These writers do compassionately chart the course of individual suffering and the painful process of individuation. The trajectory of woman's development in to a subject—from the devoiced woman placed in the master-slave dialectic to the full-fledged individual who writes herself into the hegemonic discourse and reaches the dialogic level of utterance—is carefully delineated. But they do not stop with laudatory accounts of the singular, achiever woman. Woman is redefined as an individual and as the member of a community within a womanist epistemology and woman bonding is encoded in a strategy which deconstructs patriarchal logic. This strategy is informed by an ethics of love and inclusion. Herethics, thus, can be seen immanent in the textual strategy of their narratives.

In the Indian context, the relationship between mother and daughter is more inclusive and thus demands a more comprehensive study. In the large, extended families, before the advent of the nuclear families, mothering was not strictly biological. In our cultural milieu, customary epithets, with subsumed notions of closeness, love and authority, added to relational designations gave great depth and meaning to relationships. Thus all elder females in a family became surrogate mothers and a girl child who lived in the closed female space happened to have many mothers. There was a mutual, reciprocal quality of caring in such relationships, which led to a strong sense of identification among them. Nancy Chodorow's observations about the nature of female relationships, based on her study of three different groups—working class mothers and daughters in East London, women in Javanese families and in Atjehnese families in Indonesia—are relevant in the Indian context also. She says: "The ethnographies do not imply that women are weighed down by the burden of their relationships or by overwhelming guilt and responsibility. On the contrary, they seem to have developed a strong sense of self and self-worth." (*Feminism and Psychoanalytic Theory* 61)

The nurture of daughters in patriarchy involves a profound kind of love but it is radically different from the male version of mother love. Adrienne Rich conceptualizes this love as 'courageous mothering' which can help the daughter metamorphose from an immanence into a transcendence.

The most notable fact that culture imprints on women is the sense of our limits. The most important thing one woman can do for another is to illuminate and expand her sense of actual possibilities. For a mother, this means more than contending with the reductive images of females. . . . It means that the mother herself is trying to expand the limits of her life. To refuse to be a victim: and go on from there. (*Of Woman Born* 246)

It is this courageous mothering that makes Satyabati, the protagonist of *Pratham Pratishruti*, different from the average woman and mother of her time. Satya's love for her daughter Subarna is not tainted by sympathy for the future plight of her daughter. It is not the victimized mother's identification with the daughter's future victimization. Satya refuses to be a victim and fights to change the cycle of repetitions in to which the lives of young Bengali women, including her daughter, are woven.

At the end of *Pratham Pratishruti*, on the day of Subarna's marriage, Satyabati bows out of familial relationships and Subarna does not see her mother ever again. Satya mothers Subarna, in the strictly physical sense of the word, only for nine short years. She is not the 'good mother', not the loving, suffering mother of the patriarchal mould. Satya rather symbolizes the Kristevan paradigm of good mothering. Julia Kristeva's notions about good mothering are radically different from the conventional ones. She believes that ethics is not related to duty or the idea that women should people the race. Motherhood is not an ethical duty or role. In an interview with Rosalind Coward, she says:

> Nobody knows what the good-enough mother is. I wouldn't try to explain what that is, but I would try to suggest that maybe the good-enough mother is the mother who has some things else to love besides her child, it could be her work, her husband, her lovers etc. If for a mother the child is the meaning of her life, it is too heavy. She has to have another meaning in her life. (qtd *Ethics, Politics and Difference* 88)

Satya repudiates conventional mothering and finds her meaning in life in educating women and raising their consciousness. But the physical absence of her mother fails to obliterate the traces of the maternal from Subarna's mind and to create an emotional distance. Satya is present in her mind as her aesthetics, courage, self-respect, will power, political and social alertness and sense of justice. This voice is Subarna's inheritance and it empowers her to gaze longingly beyond domesticity, with its dual chores of housework and reproduction, to see the widening horizons.

Subarna has inherited her mother's intellectual acumen, but her life is more stifling than that of Satya and naturally her acts of resistance involve more pain and more heartbreak. She needs a space where she can be herself without having demands made on her. In the introduction to the English translation of the novel, the translator, Gopa Majumdar says, "The freedom that Subarna craved showed itself in her desire for a roadside balcony on the south, a projection outside the "four walls", from where she can stay in touch with the real world, the world of action outside the household." (*Subarnalatha* ix) She craves to connect herself with the universe, to look at the stars, to feel the rays of the sun on her face and hair, to soak in the cool light of the moon. These cravings make Subarna different but difference, in the eyes of her affinal family, is equivalent to madness.

Subarna's transgressions reiterate the truth that she has inherited her mother's fierce spirit of independence and fearlessness. Everything that makes her different, her craving to reach out to the world outside, her idealism, patriotism and political alertness, her love of books and hankering for self-expression, her respect for human dignity and culture, all speak about a powerful presence in her psyche which urges her on. An irate Muktakeshi often wonders, "Will a thorn bush yield mango fruits?" (16)

Satya's influence is most powerfully felt in Subarna's courage to defy the conventional definitions of womanhood and the societal pressure which forces woman to play the roles of wife and mother as per the patriarchal agenda. Subarna has only contempt for the dictum which enjoins woman to worship her husband however mean or bad or degenerate he is and is not prepared to play the role of the *pativrata*. She has a very strict sense of right and wrong, just and unjust and does not hesitate to expose the meanness and dishonesty of Prabodh on many occasions. Unfortunately Subarna's sense of right and wrong is not compatible with that of the hypocritical society, which doles out justice based on gender. So she is blamed as a shameless woman who lacks 'womanly qualities'.

Adrienne Rich observes that the woman who reunites with her mother is breaking the social taboos which prevent women from being comrades, co-creators and co-inspirators. (*Of Woman Born* 255) Satya has bestowed on her daughter the ability to challenge the taboos and to become a co-inspirator in the great task of consciousness raising. The most inalienable asset she has left for her daughter is the selflessness, which can embrace and empathise with all the victimized and oppressed of the world. Subarna is the daughter of a mother who has fought and wept not for her Subarna alone, but for the thousands of Subarnas of Bengal. Both the mother and the daughter believe that no woman is free until the majority of women are free.

The agonized questions of the nine-year-old child as to why she was so heartlessly forsaken are answered years later by her mother in a letter. Satya's letter magically wipes away the gap of forty years and Subarna once again feels that she is sitting in her mother's lap listening to her, sharing a psychic space with her. The letter reunites an unusual daughter with her unusual, long lost mother. It defies the conventional notions of mothering because it is an epistolary enquiry into the plight of the Bengali brahmin woman. Conventional greetings and personal enquiries are conspicuously absent. But with deep, intuitive understanding Satya looks into Subarna's pain filled soul and talks to her about Hindu conjugality and the position of women in the intensely patriarchal brahmin society. She writes:

> Dear Subarna, I have not wept only for my little girl. My heart has bled for each one of those thousands of Subarnas who, I know, are held captive like you by their own cruel destiny. . . . Although I have not seen you since you were nine, I know in my heart that you have often thought the same things, that you have tried to improve not just your own situation but also that of others. (*Subarnalatha* 160)

Subarna is thrilled to the deepest core of her being because her mother's voice substantiates the rightness of her life-long struggle in a system where conjugality is synonymous with heteronomy and adds meaning to her very existence.

Perhaps, if Satya had written a letter enquiring after her husband, children and domesticity, it would have shattered an idol in her mind. But now she feels healed and excited because each word in the letter creates an empathizing vibration in her heart and each thought conflates with an identical thought in her mind. The way they relate the nation's independence to the individual's emancipation from patriarchal, hegemonic power relations and political freedom to economic and spiritual freedom foregrounds astonishingly similar perceptions. In her discussions with Ambika Kumar, the freedom fighter, Subarna vehemently argues against the male notions of nationalism and independence which excludes women from its purview. She is fiercely patriotic but she argues that while the females of this country are incarcerated by meaningless customs, the country will not be free in the true sense of the word even if it becomes politically independent. Satya's words throb with the same moral anger and indefatigable optimism when she says, "One day, every man will have to accept that women are not inferior in any way". (160)

This exceptionally strong similarity in their priorities speak about the unsevered maternal ties that defy spatial and temporal distances and of a bonding which empowers woman to demand and gain a different societal system based on a new ethics. Ashapurna Devi thus places her first mother-daughter pair in dialogic relation with the community of women in Bengal. They are preoccupied with the fate and future of women and their thoughts are focused on the community of women. Personal happiness or unhappiness seldom finds any space in their thoughts. Thus they become symbols of herethical transcendence. This capacity to outgrow narrow personalism is not merely a figment of poetic imagination as substantiated by the story of Rukhmabai. Rukhmabai, a young woman in Bombay, had approached the Bombay High Court in 1885 arguing that a marriage, even a *Hindu* marriage, was not binding on a spouse who had not consented to it. She had suffered the "unnamable miseries entailed by the custom of early marriage". But personal suffering motivated her to do something to alleviate the pain of her collective. Sudhir Chandra observes:

> Alive to the injustice of her suffering, the future rebel was able to discern in personal tragedy the predicament of her sisterhood. Self-suffering was leading to an awareness of a cheerless womanhood. . . . This saved her from consuming self-pity. She could see fellow-victims all around. The personal and the general—the existential and the political--coalesced. Her sufferings were also 'our suffering' and her fight was a larger fight. (*Enslaved Daughters* 18)

Rukhmabai's example speaks about woman's faith in herethics, an ethics that binds her to her collective by love, not by rules. It is this herethics that endows Satya and Subarna with the ability to resist the temptation to wallow in self-pity and to examine personal suffering objectively in the context of the collective.

In Ashapurna Devi's trilogy, the maternal, semiotic realm with its drives expands to include the woman of the third generation in its embrace. Subarna bows out of her life only after awakening the relentless questioning spirit in her daughter Bakul. Bakul is brought up by a mother who lacks the proverbial motherliness characterized by forbearance and sweetness of temper. But this defiant, unconventional mother is the most persistent presence in Bakul's memory and thoughts. Speaking about the inalienable assets handed over by the mother to the daughter, Adrienne Rich says: "The quality of the mother's life--however embattled and unprotected--is her primary bequest to her daughter, because a woman who can believe in herself, who is a fighter, and who continues to struggle to create livable space around her, is demonstrating to her daughter that these possibilities exist." (*Of Woman Born* 247). Bakul knows that all the battles and all the bitterness were for creating livable space for girls like her. This knowledge prompts her to search into the past to see the women written out of history.

Young Bakul used to feel embarrassed by the emotional outbursts of her mother. Gradually she learns the art of observing things with the detached, but understanding eyes of an intelligent spectator. She reads and understands the signs of resistance, defiant gestures of non-compliance and protest against cultural prescriptions that make her mother different from many of her fellow women. She realizes that her mother "had high hopes about human values and great expectations about the world. She wanted to unite the creatures called human beings with the true meaning of the term human." (*Bakulinte katha*, 74, my translation)

Bakul is able to empathise with Subarna's intense longing for self-expression because of a similar, creative spark in her own heart and after Subarna's death, Bakul searches for the manuscript of *Smriti Katha* but it is irrevocably lost.

Then she makes a promise to her mother and grandmother. She vows that she will write their story and recreate the saga of women's resistance in Bengal.

But the transformation from Bakul to Anamika Devi, the famous writer, is not an easy one. She has the burden of a broken love to bear. Her father and brothers conveniently forget that in their tradition-loving brahmin family, a girl is still unmarried. Bakul knows how selfish her father has become, but considers it a blessing in disguise. Thus the binding chains of tradition slips away and Bakul becomes Anamika. As always, there is strong resistance from the men in the family. They try to suppress her struggles for creativity and identity. But Bakul succeeds where Subarna had failed. She does not raise her voice in anger, but smiles sarcastically. She stands erect with calm dignity facing the accusing stares of her father and brothers and establishes her right to do what she thinks is right. In Bakul we see the woman who actualizes her potential and challenges the system from within. Julia Kristeva believes that as women are less forcibly separated from their mothers and less integrated in the patriarchal culture, they can enter the symbolic order and at the same time call it into question. Ashapurna Devi substantiates the veracity of the argument in the creation of Bakul.

Even though Anamika is an eagerly welcomed presence in the academic and intellectual circles, she never revels in her privileged singularity. She is in perfect communion with the innumerable, unknown women. She tells them, "I am yours. I write to express the innermost thoughts of your mind." (37, my translation) Thus Anamika becomes the link between the past and the present. She narrates the stories of the past to remind the women of the new generation how much they all owe to the grandmothers and mothers, the pioneering women. At the same time the contemporaneity of her thoughts bridges distances between her and the present. Thus she becomes the symbol of the new woman who reaches back to the old and reaches out to the young generations to create a community of women across temporal, spatial and emotional distances.

Nabankur: The Seedling's Tale captures the multiple dimensions of the mother-daughter bonding, but its focus is on the love that permits separation. *Nabankur* is the story of a girl child's journey to adulthood and autonomy. The protagonist, Chhobi, is rooted in her relationship with her mother and the other women of her family. She draws sustenance from the bonding even as she reaches out for light. As a seedling she cannot remain in the earth forever because it would mean not coming to life at all. At the same time, to be uprooted entirely would mean withering before reaching the prime. The seedling can grow and come to fruition only when there is perfect symbiosis between the roots that go deep into the soil and the leaves that open to the sunlight. Thus the narrative is centred in a mother-daughter bond which is characterized by the ability to let go. Discussing the interstices of the mother-daughter relationship, Nancy Friday observes:

> Letting go is perhaps a friendlier way to put it. It implies generosity, a talent good mother needs in abundance. Separation is not loss, it is not cutting yourself off from someone you love. It is giving freedom to the other person to be herself before she becomes resentful, stunted, and suffocated by being tied too close. Separation is not the end of love. It creates love. (*My Mother/Myself* 91)

This irony is foregrounded by Mamata and Chhobi, the mother and daughter in *Nabankur*.

Chhobi resists her family's efforts to carve and chisel her in to a sexed form, and so is reprimanded and humiliated by the elders. Even her innocent transgressions like the urge to learn or to play with the boys are seen as a threat to the established norms. They cannot allow her to violate the prescriptions of womanhood which is the fate of a Bengali high caste woman. Chhobi sees this fate crystallized in the form of the women around her. But she is too much of a rebel to succumb to the pressures that prevent a girl from achieving any sense of her self.

Mamata, Chhobi's mother and the woman of the earlier generation, is not completely unawakened, but succumbs to her destiny and conforms to the very orthodox ways of her conjugal family. She gives up the accomplishments that mark her as different, her love for music and books, and gets chained to domesticity and femininity. But certain embers are kept consciously, painstakingly alive in her mind to light the path for her daughter to walk out of the system that has devoured the mother. In the introduction to *Nabankur*, Himani Bannerjee says:

> Chhobi's mother in particular stands as a reminder of the punishment that the patriarchal script holds for women. And yet the desire of growing up, of becoming active in the world and of being creative is not fully crushed in her. They are literally embodied by and infused in to her daughter, and expressed in the child's own longing for outward bound movement, education, creativity and independence. (xv)

In the core of her being, Mamata is not ashamed of being a woman and so she will not allow her daughter to be ashamed of femaleness or to be immanent. She symbolises Adrienne Rich's concept of good mothering. Speaking about mother-daughter relationship and the mother's role in moulding the female child, Rich argues, "A woman who feels pride in being female will not visit her self-depreciation upon her female child." (*Of Woman Born* 245)

Mamata knows that Chhobi is tougher, braver and more intelligent than her son and the other boys in the family. But she also knows that these qualities would make her little daughter's life unbearable within the confined, confining spaces of the very orthodox household. So she takes the crucial decision to send her away with Sukumari, her sister-in-law, to the town where she can do her schooling. For a woman whose heart aches with an ineffable pain when she looks at the eager, intelligent face of her little daughter, for one who pours out all the unexpressed love by hugging the sleeping form of the child at night, when nobody watches, this decision is a painful one. But Mamata is prepared to bear the pain of separation for Chhobi's sake. Her intense, selfless love for Chhobi empowers her to leave the margins and occupy the core position to intervene on behalf of her daughter because, as Nancy Friday observes, "The truly loving mother is one whose interest and happiness is in seeing her daughter as a person, not just as a possession." (*My Mother/ Myself* 69)

The narrative is silent about one crucial aspect of Mamata's decision and the silence invites the reader to probe in to the psychodynamics of bonding and separation. Mamata is the devoiced, invisibilised bride of the Ray family and has no agency in the decision-making process. Even Purnasashi, her mother-in-law, does not have the authority to make decisions even though she has to implement the male decisions in the women's quarters. In this context, the very idea of a woman negotiating for a space for her daughter and making the decision to keep her away from the lien of the family is definitely a transgressive act. All the more importantly, her transgression does not meet with much resistance from her in laws. The reason for this unprecedented, unexpected lack of resistance can be found in the unhappy destiny of another daughter.

Sukumari, Dakshinaranjan Ray's eldest daughter, is married to a rich businessman and has everything in life but the stigma of the barren woman cast shadows over all the other fortunes. The family must definitely be aware of her loneliness and her longing for a child and so when Mamata proposes to send Chhobi with Sukumari, it must be a welcome thought to the Rays. Thus Mamata makes a very intelligent move on behalf of Chhobi. But it has its risks also, as she must definitely know, because there is always the possibility of Sukumari turning possessive and luring the child away from her mother. Moreover the very rich ambience of Sukumari's home combined with the freedom that town life can give might change Chhobi's attitude to life and relationships. But Mamata is prepared to take the risks to help her daughter attain personhood even if it creates emotional and spatial distances between the mother and the daughter. Perhaps she knows, with the unerring instinct of the strong mother, that distances are temporary and that the mutual respect of two women, who can assert their identity even as they cherish a symbiotic relationship with each other, can close in the gaps. Thus Mamata challenges the conventional definitions of motherhood and stands as the symbol of good mothering as conceptualized by feminist thinkers and psychoanalysts.

Chhobi comes back from her aunt's house after eight long years as a soft-spoken beautiful young woman and Mamata sees her young self in Chhobi. But Chhobi is determined to map out a future which is different from her mother's past and present. The soft gaze and the gentle voice hide a fearless mind. The transgressions of the young woman are too serious to be ignored, but her father and grandfather are helpless in the presence of an incredibly strong determination, which they have always considered to be a male prerogative. After Chhobi's ultimate transgression of refusing to marry the man chosen for her by the family, when the atmosphere is fraught with tension, Mamata intervenes once again and makes arrangements for her daughter to make her tryst with destiny. Coming from a woman who had killed her talents and dreams for fear of annoying the conjugal family, this intervention does indeed foreground courageous mothering. Mamata proves that love can make a mother strong enough to question marginality.

Unlike the ordinary mothers of the time, Mamata dares to envisage a different, bigger future for her daughter and so she takes a brave decision. She will not allow her fears and anxieties to affect Chhobi's confidence. She knows perfectly well that her daughter is in no way inferior to the men in the family, but has a premonition that she has a lot of sorrow in store for her. The system has no space for a free spirit like Chhobi. Still Mamata arranges for Chhobi to go to Calcutta and to join a college there. The decision requires immense courage because Calcutta is far away from the little village of Kusumpur and Mamata's cousin, with whom Chhobi is to stay, is practically a stranger. But Mamata has faith in her daughter's capacity to struggle and to survive.

Not surprisingly, Chhobi inherits her mother's courage and the willingness to let go. Her love for Tamal, a young man who belongs to another caste, is so deep that it is a constant ache within her, but she knows that the poor, jobless Tamal, burdened with family responsibilities may not be able to keep the promises made to her. She will go on even if Tamal fails to walk with her. She will not blame him or try to keep him for herself. "No, Chhobi was not going to hold anyone in bondage. She pledged to herself that she would never stand in anyone's way, she would never allow herself to be weak" (*Nabankur* 241). Thus the mother and daughter prove that bonding is not bondage.

The mother-daughter dyads analysed so far bring out the complex and rich responses that motherhood can evoke in daughters. They are also celebrations of the personhood of the mother without which motherhood is not complete. These mothers and daughters share a consciousness about their status as human beings, the urge to strive for autonomy and awareness about the socio-political and cultural milieu in which they are situated.

In this context, another dimension of the relationship, which is marked by a set of polarities like awakened-unawakened, fearful-fearless and transcendent-immanent, need be explored. The mother here is an essentializing signifier of femininity and hence cannot, apparently, exert any influence on her daughter who is defiant. But the interaction between the contrasted pair, Bhuvaneswari and Satyabati in *Pratham Pratishruti* focuses on the possibility of durability within fragility and power within powerlessness. It proves that even though these mothers are silent and invisible otherwise, their presences are powerfully affirmed in their daughters' lives. The conforming mother, thus, proves to be the first person to motivate the non-conforming daughter's thought processes.

Bhuvaneswari, Satya's mother in *Pratham Pratishruti*, symbolises a silenced, unawakened consciousness. Fear is the dominant emotion that rules her narrow existence and Ashapurna Devi's narrative contrasts the images of fear and fearlessness in the portrayal of the mother and daughter. Bhuvaneswari is the eldest daughter-in-law of the richest brahmin family in Nityanandapur and the wife of a very powerful man, but she never tries to assert her rightful place and never articulates any suggestions or questions and thus, like Gayatri Chakravorty Spivak's female subaltern, is written out of the male canon. She is afraid of the elders of her conjugal family, of social customs and of God. She is fear stricken when her defiant daughter transgresses the boundaries and becomes the object of severe criticism. Above all she is afraid of her husband who is so aloof that she cannot even dream of taking any freedom with him. Ultimately it is fear that causes her death at a very young age because even when she is stricken by cholera, she does not dare to inform her husband, the most famous doctor in the area, and to seek his help.

Satya, the spirited, rebellious daughter is initially indifferent to her timid mother, but when first marriage and then death alienates her from her mother permanently, her thoughts persistently come back to the gentle, unassuming woman. She now knows that a girl's childhood is a treasure locked up in her mother's heart and that she can be a child once again, experience the sense of belonging in her natal home, only as long as her mother is alive.

As a child she is puzzled by fear, which is epitomized by her mother, and the faces of an ever-fearful mother and a fearless daughter float up before her inner eyes repeatedly. She enters on a quest to know the reason and the meaning of the fear that controls and confines women's life. She locates it in ignorance and her life becomes a battle against the patriarchal power which keeps women unlettered and ignorant. Satya finds fulfillment in teaching women and guiding them to autonomy.

The two contrastive signifiers of womanhood, the mother and the daughter, are linked through memory and at every stage of her life, Satya remembers her mother and wonders how life would have been different if she, and other women like her, had the awareness and opportunity to break the killing bonds of fear. At the time of her ultimate transgression of leaving her family, she refuses her patrimony and tells her husband that if her sons grow up as human beings, they should use it to establish a school for women and name it Bhuvaneswari Vidyalaya. It is interesting that she does not name it after her father who is a renowned scholar. The school becomes a success and gives light to scores of women and thus Satya writes her mother's name permanently into history. The mother-daughter relationship thus shows how even an ordinary mother can be a potentially transforming force in her daughter's life.

The idea of the continuity between mothers and daughters reveals the links that reach beyond the mothers to the grandmothers and great-grandmothers. The assertion of the genealogy of women within the family thus becomes an emerging strategy. The narratives of Ashapurna Devi and Sulekha Sanyal are situated within a dialectic of female ancestries and they subvert the established notions about generation gaps. The perfect communion among women energizes and empowers them to bridge the temporal and emotional gaps and become fellow workers in a common cause.

The absence of empathy between the first and third generations, between the grandmother and the granddaughter, can create serious fissures in the female genealogy as demonstrated by the Tamil novelist, Sivasankari, in her novel *Palangal* [Bridges]. In this, even the thinking woman who fights against the social system as a young wife and a mother, fails to understand her granddaughter's urge for autonomy. She fails to recognize the inherent principle of movement within change and insists that the younger generation should be satisfied with the changes the older generation has managed to bring about. The relationship between the grandmother and granddaughter is fraught with tension because there is no mutual understanding. They belong to two different worlds and the mother has to function as the bridge to keep them from drifting away from each other completely.

Ashapurna Devi's novel, *Pratham Pratishruti*, on the other hand, speaks about the bonds that fill generation gaps. The novel begins with the famous pronouncement: "I did not make up Satyabati's story. I took it from Bakul's notebook." (*First Promise* 1). By narrating the story of her grandmother Satyabati, Bakul is paying a debt to all those pioneering women who had fought to create a world of openness and freedom. "The shadow dark waters of a pool in some secluded village overflow in the monsoon to join the river and gush forth in torrents. That same river rushes along, and one day joins the ocean. We must never forget that initial flowing forth out of the shadows" (2). Bakul acknowledges the significance of that first drop of water that flowed out of the little village pool and thereby fulfills the promise made to the memory of her dead mother.

Bakul's notebook is obviously her creative genius and it is enriched by a blood stream of inheritance. She lives in the physical and emotional presence of her mother for sixteen years and comes to understand her fully in the last few months of her life. So when she writes Subarna's life it does not come about as a surprise. But when Bakul painstakingly collects each and every detail of her grandmother's life and recreates an unusual woman who would otherwise have remained unknown, it bespeaks of a very deep and strong bonding. She studies the history of the years of struggle of mothers, grandmothers and great-grandmothers. "Therefore, the Satyabati she has never held with her eyes, she has seen in her dreams and imaginings, and regarded her with compassion and admiration. Satyabati's portrait is clearly etched in Bakul's notebook" (2).

Satya is never an openly acknowledged memory in young Bakul's life because her name has been a taboo in Bakul's house. But any exploration into the troubled existence of Subarna is sure to bring Satya's latent presence to the surface, and thus Bakul enters Satya's life through Subarna. Satya is reborn in Bakul's creative mind and grows there, lives each day of her life till the last day when she walks out from Subarna's life. But it is not merely a chronological account of a woman's life. With incisive understanding, Bakul recreates the hegemonic power relations embedded in the familial and social structure of Satya's day, and more importantly, probes into Satya's mind to bring out the psycho-dynamics of resistance. Thus Bakul achieves the difficult, but fulfilling, task of sharing a psychic space with her ancestor, whom her physical eyes have never seen, and invests the term 'bonding' with its total, ultimate meaning.

In *Nabankur*, Chhobi's relationship with her grandmother passes through problematic, troubled phases to reach the serene stage of mutual understanding. Purnasashi is the typical, patriarchal woman who is moulded in such a way that she fails to empathise with her own community. As an insignificant girl child and later as a child bride, she had been brushed aside indifferently. Any attention centred on her would usually precede cruel, merciless disciplinary moves. The pain and the anger walled up in her psyche sours into intolerance and thus Purnasashi, the grandmother, actively dislikes Chhobi's urge to individuate.

Chhobi is initially angry and upset about her grandmother's prejudices because she is too young to understand the psycho-dynamics of oppression. But later, the eighteen-year old, educated Chhobi consciously probes the patriarchal system that makes weapons out of women to curb the seedling's attempt to reach out to the sky. With great patience, she follows the trajectory of Purnasashi's life and understands how women's ignorance is exploited to keep them away from one another. Chhobi's resentment is replaced by compassion and marks the beginning of an enriching relationship.

Purnasashi, as the unawakened woman of the earlier generation, cannot approve of all the transgressions of her granddaughter, but she finds herself unwittingly blessing the child when she moves out of the confines of the orthodox household. The distance between the Purnasashi who strongly believes that marriage is the ultimate destination and destiny of a woman's life and Purnasashi who sees her granddaughter off with prayers for her future is remarkable. This distance is traversed by the grandmother and the granddaughter together.

In the novels under study, the patriarchal ethics of submission to law is replaced by herethics of love and a community of women comes into being. The grandmother-granddaughter symbiosis initiates an inductive movement into the change that comes over the relationships among women when influenced by a potential subject. The reader is made to travel with the protagonists from childhood to old age and to see that Satya, in *Pratham Pratishruti*, and Subarna, in *Subarnalatha*, do not become as callous, ill-tempered and narrow-minded as their respective mothers-in-law. There is a psychic osmosis between the older and the younger generations and the women of the older generation do not revert to the role of the elder women, who were weapons in the hands of the patriarchs, of their time. In the earlier context, when women did not have the opportunity to think or decide for themselves, the story of oppression was a continuum. The most cruelly treated child bride later became the cruellest mother-in-law. The pain and the humiliations suppressed within were unleashed on the young women who were objects of their mercy. But when women are educated and encouraged to develop their thinking and rationalizing powers, they recognize the patriarchal strategy of defining women in relation with men, thereby sowing the seeds of insecurity, suspicion and competition in their minds. When they realise that they are, first and foremost, human beings, they can see beyond role definitions and so do not feel threatened by one another. Thus one woman's presence can bring comfort and jouissance to the other.

In the community of women, relationships do not necessarily develop unidirectionally from grandmother to mother to daughter. Even as a girl's existence is deeply embedded in the bloodstream of the mother and grandmother, her roots run in different directions towards other blood and kinship relations, giving her a sense of belonging within her community. Nancy Chodorow observes that the children who grow up in collective child-rearing situations, without exclusive mothering, "develop more sense of solidarity and commitment to the group, less individualism and competitiveness." (*The Reproduction of Mothering* 217) In the extended families, equations like senior-junior and own-other mark the relationships among the female family core. But one common and congruent feature which underlies them all is the nurturer-nurtured equation, which defies the own-other equation. This is keenly felt in communities which are familiar with non-biological mothering.

Negotiations between children and older women, especially in the joint family system prevalent in the different provinces of India, are embedded in non-biological mothering and so aunts nurturing nieces is a common experience. In many cases, the relationship has limited scope because it is part of the daily chores of women to feed, bathe and dress children. The children and the older women love one another, but it does not always develop into deeper understanding. But in the novels analyzed here, the aunt-niece relationship is not confined to mere nurturance, but grows into a higher dimension, where it functions as a mutually enlightening and empowering bond.

In *Pratham Pratishruti*, Satya's relationship with Mokshada, her aunt, is initially strained by Mokshada's unflinching stance as the champion of brahminical, patriarchal system and Satya's role as the eternal rebel who defiantly interrogates the infallibility of the system and so there is an emotional distance between them. Young Satyabati's interactions with the world of the patriarchal women are marked with anger and contempt because she is acutely aware of the paradox of women victimizing women. She impatiently challenges the system, but does not understand that any reconstruction involves an inward movement to reach the root cause that makes woman both a victim and a weapon.

The grown up Satya is wiser, more experienced and can now see into the naked souls of the women around her and sense the palpable fear that turn women against one another. As a woman, Satya now sees the negations and denials in Mokshada's life and understands how she has been cheated out of life. She now knows that the deep wounds inflicted on the mind of a helpless child widow who had never seen or known her husband, who had never known the meaning of marriage, can fester and turn toxic permeating each living thought and action. She also knows that when one, who had never had any happiness in life tries to kill other people's happiness, she deserves sympathy, not hatred.

But what is more important and more enriching is the attitudinal change that comes over Mokshada. Satya's decision to go to Calcutta with her husband and sons would have angered the Mokshada of the past because Satya is challenging the age-old joint family system. She would also have worried about Satya and her children losing caste. But the Mokshada of the present is happy for her niece's success and admits something she would never have admitted to anyone else: "It is true Satya. All my life I have lashed out at you. I used to think you'd have a hard time. Now I see that you're the winner." (*First Promise* 298)

Without any envy or malice, the older woman sees the younger one off to make her signature in life. Mokshada's change can be attributed to the presence of Satya who, as the woman who has transcended to subjecthood, makes an impact on the life of her community. Her urge to seek the ultimate meaning of woman's life and her attempt to interrogate the existing system, inspire women like Mokshada to subject their own lives into a rethinking. Even the tiny spark in Mokshada's consciousness is vitally important because, even though an old woman like her will never take any active role in resistance, she will bless the subject and strengthen her resolve to continue to fight. Such female relationships motivate the luckier woman to study the privileged-non-privileged equation objectively and to see the privileged position not as an exclusive right but as an invitation and an initiation into a quest for better opportunities for all in the community.

In *Bakulkatha*, Ashapurna Devi once again employs the contrasted pair to foreground yet another facet of aunt-niece relationship. Overtly any bonding between Bakul and her niece, Shampa, seems to be unlikely because the dissimilarities in their demeanors are strikingly present while similarities are conspicuously absent. But still, the serious, reticent Bakul and the frivolous, talkative Shampa share a psychic space which enables them to develop a strong bonding marked with mutual respect and admiration. Nurturing is never a part of their relationship but love definitely is. The relationship between them is that of the creator of history and the writer of history. The unassuming Bakul considers her transgressions more as accidents than acts of will and so she has great admiration for the fighters and achievers of both the older and younger generations, represented by Satya, Subarna and Shampa.

Shampa is the one person in the family who dares to barge into Bakul's private domain unannounced and her boisterous presence is not confined to the room. Her presence is a very loud one in Bakul's mind and it stimulates the creative writer's thought processes by placing herself side by side with the women of earlier generations. Bakul is plagued by doubts about the pace and the nature of the changes that challenge everything that is old as foolish and obsolete but she never attempts to make value judgments about the thoughts and actions of others. She knows that the values of one generation are worthless for another generation and that only Time can be the ultimate judge. There are times when Bakul is exasperated by Shampa's uncontrollable tongue and her lack of respect for all and everything. But this does not affect their mutual love. Bakul admires the fearlessness of Shampa while Shampa respects the quiet dignity of Bakul. Theirs is an understanding, which can reach beyond differences.

As a link in a female genealogy, Bakul knows how the fearless among them have always interrogated the system, which treats women as objects. She witnesses the cycle becoming complete now and writes Shampa into history just as she had written Satya and Subarna earlier into it. Even as she narrates Shampa's story, she is aware that she is not writing about one woman's life. She is writing about the new womanhood that refuses to be victimized. She has already written the stories of her mother and grandmother; how they had laboriously made a little mud path for the Bengali woman to tread on. Now she will write about Shampa, the charioteer.

The third aunt-niece dyad, Sukumari and Chhobi in *Nabankur*, dramatizes the concept of bonding with a curious reversal of the nurturer-nurtured roles. Chhobi, the perspicacious child, nurtures her *Baro Pishima*, Sukumari, back to emotional stability and sense of security by making her feel that she has someone and something to live for.

Sukumari is a rich man's wife but behind the glittering jewels and the soft rustling silks, there is the ugly, painful truth of denials. The pain and humiliation caused by the presence of another woman in her husband's life is accentuated by childlessness. But in her society, if a woman is unhappy in her marriage it is her fate and if she is childless, it is her fault. So the embittered Sukumari raises a huge wall of inapproachability around her and shuts her fragmented, lonely self in it. She will neither allow any one to see her wounded soul nor let the pain of others touch her.

Chhobi is initially an unwilling pawn in a power game which she does not fully understand. Sukumari wants to play the same game of denial and to inflict the same kind of pain on her husband and needs Chhobi's presence as her shield. But Chhobi refuses to become the shield behind which Sukumari can hide and becomes the bridge between her aunt and the world around her. From the beginning, she is not deceived by appearances and feels that her *Pishi*'s loud laughter somehow does not match her sleepless, tired look. With her love and compassion, she gently persuades her *Pishima* to open her tightly closed mind and empties it off the negative emotions of anger and self-pity. Her presence has a cathartic effect on Sukumari. Here Sanyal is giving expression to a love which is uncorrupted by possessiveness. When Chhobi heals the wounds of her aunt and channelises her love to the more deserving, the needier, she is making a statement of her ethics.

All relationships imply mutuality and this is true in the case of Sukumari and Chhobi also. Sukumari nurtures the wild, irrepressible girl of ten in to the serious, dignified young woman of eighteen. She provides Chhobi with every requisite essential for her growth, from dolls to the best school in the locality. But Chhobi is indebted to her aunt not merely for the material things. Sukumari opens her eyes to the possibility of the pain behind the smile. It is her *Pishima*'s unhappiness that makes Chhobi observe the world around her and see the mute suffering there. She becomes aware of caste and wealth and perceives the chasms they create in society. More importantly her *Pishima*'s life conveys to her the gendered oppression to which even a rich, high-born woman can be subjected. Thus Sukumari becomes indirectly instrumental in grooming Chhobi into a subject.

As already discussed, in patriarchal societies female relationships are generally ignored. But there are some relationships which are completely unrecognized. In the Indian context, friendship between sisters-in-law and more crucially, between co-wives are perceived to be non-existent. The misinterpretations around them are so dense that people fail to see them. As Laura E. Donaldson, while discussing Ralph Ellison's novel, *Invisible Man* and the issue of the invisibility of the underdog says, "Seeing or not seeing is a paradigmatic and hermeneutic act". (*Decolonising Feminisms* 13) She argues that racial, economic and gendered segregations can place some people in a social transparency where others refuse to see them: "The true failure, then, is that of the inner eye—the hermeneutic eye--which selects some random elements of reality and foreground them as meaningful patterns but relegates others to a meaningless background" (14). It is precisely this failure of the hermeneutic eye that has always problematised the relationships among sisters-in-law and among co-wives. Jealousy and rivalry, which are by-products of emotional and financial insecurity, had very often turned such relationships sour but it was only one aspect of reality and so to treat them as absolutely non-existent cannot be justified. The works of Ashapurna Devi and Sulekha Sanyal are influential on redefining and visibilising them.

The blood-stream of inheritance that cathects mothers and daughters, grandmothers and granddaughters, aunts and nieces and sisters with one another is absent in the case of sisters-in-law, but that does not prevent them from understanding each other and from sharing their vision.

The strategy of the male narratives that places sisters by marriage in the self-other positions is conspicuously absent in the novels under study. For example Satyabati and Saudamini in *Pratham Pratishruti* are different from each other, but they are not opposites. Satya challenges the Hindu conjugal order and leaves the family while Sadu takes the initiative to retrieve her long-lost conjugal status. Their experiences in and responses to life are different. Satya craves for freedom from familial and social hierarchies while Sadu seeks shelter and happiness within its folds. But they do not sit in judgment over the perspectives or actions of each other. One will not emulate the other, but that does not stop them from admiring each other.

Sadu is a rejected wife and so is reduced to the status of a slave and treated as a non-entity. Satya is astonished by the infinite patience and forbearance with which she faces the filthy, caustic verbosity of Elokeshi, but she knows that behind the cheerful façade, there are the unhealed wounds caused by rejection. So when Sadu breaks the silence of many years and writes to Mukund Mukherji, her husband, giving him a chance to renew the relationship, Satya is unhappy but not angry. She has moved far ahead of the unawakened multitudes, but does not shut herself up in her privileged position. Her thoughts are persistently with her community and thus she can see in to the workings of the mind of a woman who is forced to remember every waking minute of her life that she is an unwanted appendage. She can understand Sadu's need to be loved, to be wanted, to have a space of her own. Moreover she respects Sadu for steering the course of her life, even though their paths are different.

In her own way, Sadu proves to be of immense importance to Satya because this unlettered village woman provides her emotional anchor with her undemanding, unconditional love when Satya's life becomes turbulent. From the very beginning, she is the only person in Satya's affinal home who tries to understand her. She is the nine-year-old bride's companion and confidante and is invited to share the innermost thoughts and urges that drive her on. Of course,

Sadu is not awakened enough to understand the significance of the changes that occur around her and Satya's role in it, but she is sure that her *thakurji* is an unusual person and also that Nabakumar's family is not worthy of her.

It is significant that Ashapurna Devi chooses Sadu as Satya's companion on the fateful day when Subarna is given in marriage without Satya's knowledge. She is the only person who is not blind to the tortured soul of Satya and unlike Nabakumar is sensitive to the excruciating pain behind the hard decision of renouncing family. In that crucial moment Sadu severs her ties with tradition, symbolized by Nabakumar's family and declares her solidarity with the woman who openly defies her family and society. Sadu's last words to Satya are extremely important because they throb with a multitude of emotions like love, respect, anxiety, tenderness and awe. When she learns that Satya plans to earn her living by teaching women she says: "I'm older than you and I'm not supposed to touch your feet, but that's just what I feel like doing" (*First Promise* 534). Sadu's gesture marks the birth of a woman who is ready to reject the deeply internalized ideology of female dependence.

One particular pair of sisters by marriage, Subarna and her second sister-in-law Subala, in *Subarnalatha*, stands apart from the others mentioned here because of a unique emotional and spiritual compatibility that makes one the extension of the other. The depth of the relationship is revealed by the fact that Subala is the only person Subarna longs to see while she is in her deathbed.

Unlike the other children of Muktakeshi, Subala is capable of thinking beyond caste, gender and wealth. And also unlike others, she is not blind to the psychodynamics of resistance and the craving for political freedom that are rising in tremendous waves in the world around her. She loves people for what they are, not for what custom demands them to be. To her the lives of girls are more valuable than caste and the honour of the family and so she does not hesitate to give her daughters in marriage to young men of different castes. She will not allow poverty and caste to ruin their lives. She is perfectly aware of the fact that her family has virtually cast her out for this transgression, but is not worried about it as her words indicate: "I know none of you like the idea, but my girls are very happy in their homes. Frankly, that's all I care about." (*Subarnalatha* 202)

These are the qualities that endear Subala to Subarna, even as they distance her from others of her natal family. In Subala Subarna sees a kindred spirit, one who thinks and acts just as she would have done if her situation were different. The last exchange between the two women stresses the perfect understanding between them. Subala looks at Subarna's thin pale face and the dark eyes now sunk deep into their sockets and says, "I think *Mejo Bou*, if you were not a woman, imprisoned in your own home, you would have left these four walis and go. Like Ambika, you would have set out to see the world". Subarna's reply is filled with love and pain because no one had ever tried to understand her. "Thakurji . . . How is it that you know me so well? How many times have you met me? How do you know what I think and what I feel?" (203) Ashapurna Devi thus portrays the tenderest and deepest relationships among women through Subarna and Subala repudiating the male construct that sisters by marriage are habitual enemies.

The relationship between the sisters-in-law in *Nabankur*, Mamata and Sukumari, is more complex because unlike Satya and Sadu, or Subarna and Subala they have the same object of love and weave different dreams around her. Mamata wants Chhobi to attain autonomy through education and transcend the life of negations, which was her mother's lot. Sukumari, on the other hand, wants Chhobi to occupy the space of the daughter she will never have and fulfill her urge to love and be loved.

There are two factors that save the relationship from souring into jealous rivalry—their unconditional love for Chhobi and the mutual understanding that runs deep within their consciousness. Obviously, they love Chhobi very much and will not allow their own petty selfishness to interfere with the future or the happiness of the girl. They understand each other and care for each other and this empathy enables them to resolve their anxieties.

Sukumari remembers her *Boudi* as the youthful, accomplished urban bride of yester years and is sentient to the unhappiness of the silent, middle-aged Mamata. Unlike the other village girls of her acquaintance, Sukumari had always wished for something more than marriage. Her vague longings and pain give her insight into the thoughts of a kindred spirit and thus she sees into Mamata's mind where dreams and desires lie shattered.

Mamata also cherishes a fund of love for her sister-in-law who was her friend in the early years of her marriage and has become almost a stranger to her natal family after marriage. While the other women of the Ray family are dazzled by Sukumari's wealth and celebrate her luck, Mamata with the unerring instinct of a close companion senses the terrible pain of shared love under which she is wilting. She is also aware of the unrelieved loneliness of the childless woman. But unlike others, including her mother, she will not accept the woman's lack of fecundity as the unquestioned, unquestionable reason for this. It is this quality of sentience that forges a bond between them which is strong enough to make them share the great task of grooming the girl child into an autonomous being. Neither tries to turn the child into her exclusive property and thus gives her the first lessons in the importance of alterity.

Friendly relationship among co-wives had earlier been kept out of male narratives as an impossibility and hence the woman writer had to take it upon herself to probe into the politics and polemics of it. Obviously when two or more women look upon the same male as the provider and master and depend on him for economic and emotional security, several factors can problematise the relationship among them. But generalizing the situation results in the naturalization of it and in the consequent failure in acknowledging the friendship and solidarity, which were definitely there.

In this context, the portrayal of co-wives by writers like Ashapurna Devi must be seen as articulations of both empirical fact and hope filled vision. She visualizes a scenario where the evolving female consciousness makes the unfortunate women who become co-wives realize that they are trapped by a system which churns out losers, without ever allowing any one of them to become winners. Once this truth dawns on them, they develop the hermeneutic eye to see one another in a new light and to empathise with their fellow losers.

In the huge canvas of *Pratham Pratishruti*, coloured by striking women characters, there are two pairs of co-wives and Ashapurna Devi employs one pair to show the absence and the other to show the presence of bonding as directly related to fragmentariness and empowerment respectively. The first pair, Sarada and Patli, speaks about deep unhealed wounds and unbridgeable gaps while the second pair, Saudamini and Mukund Mukherji's second wife, projects an inclusive friendship untainted by competition.

Sarada, like the other girls of her time, is brought up in a system that views the co-wife as a 'barb'. Satyabati animatedly tells her father how all girls are initiated in to the *sejuti* ritual, which is meant to protect them the 'barb of a co-wife'. The songs they chant are, virtually, abuses showered on the co-wife and substantiate the hatred and fear instilled into a little girl's mind. But later, if she chances to have a co-wife, she has to submit to the situation, swallowing all her anger and hurt because she has absolutely no agency in the matter. These negative emotions, which lurk just beneath the surface, erupt at the slightest provocation, disturbing the peace of the antahpuram, but later subside to resigned sulkiness.

Sarada, like all other girls, has internalized this hatred and so, quite naturally finds it difficult to accept the presence of Patli. But unlike others, she is acutely aware of her rights as a wife and so refuses to compromise with the situation. She continues to do the household chores of cooking and feeding a large family, paying special attention to individual likes and dislikes but she withdraws from dialogic, meaningful interaction with her collective.

An analysis of the reactions of Sarada and Satya in similar situations, situations in which broken promises complicate their lives, will foreground the fact that education is a determinant in their respective decisions. Sarada is deeply hurt by a broken promise, which amounts to betrayal in her eyes but she cannot walk out of the life that she now detests because of a major lack in her life. She is not educated and cannot harbour any hopes about being economically independent. The resulting dependence is too demeaning for a proud woman like her and it sours her life into one of cynical detachment. She continues to be the *Boro bou* accepting that "it is a woman's fate to build her home on the quicksand of such false vows." (*First Promise* 105) Satya reacts strongly against the broken promise and takes the decision to leave the shelter of her family and patrimony because she is confident of earning her livelihood. Thus Sarada is fragmented into a wounded heart and well-fed body and her fragmentariness remains unsolved while Satya's unified self becomes a motivating force for her community.

The second pair of co-wives in the same novel, Saudamini and Mukund Mukherji's second wife, shares a symbiotic relationship which turns non-achievers in to achievers. These two women transcend all the denials and absences in their lives and create a space for themselves by mutually helping each other.

Saudamini's experiences have taught her how heartless and selfish Mukund Mukherji is, and so instead of considering her co-wife a rival, she feels compassion for the woman. The sympathy is returned in equal measure and Sadu's co-wife believes that perhaps Sadu was her mother in another birth. Sadu teases her that a co-wife can never be like a mother, but she lavishes on her all the love she would have spent on a daughter. She is moved by her gesture which includes and gives her a share in the large family. The two women enjoy their easy friendship and find peace in each other's company. This mutual understanding is their talisman against further hurt and disappointment.

The complete absence of rivalry between co-wives is not merely an expression of female imagination. It fascinates male imagination also as substantiated by Khaled Hosseini's *A Thousand Splendid Suns.* The dual protagonists, Mariam and Laila show how deep the love between women can run and how far one will go to protect the other. The middle-aged Mariam kills her husband Rasheed to save her fourteen-year-old co-wife from a life of torture and misery. She is sentenced to death by the Taliban and dies happily without any regrets because "she was leaving the world as a woman who had loved and been loved back. She was leaving it as a friend, a companion, a guardian. A mother." (*A Thousand Splendid Suns* 329)

The concept of woman bonding is reinscribed by empirical evidence also. Jim Corbett, the legendary hunter, while narrating his experiences during his innumerable travels in the villages in the foothills of the Himalayas remembers an incident he had once witnessed. A case which has the usual triangular constituents of the besotted husband, ageing first wife, and nubile second wife is brought before the white Magistrate and the first wife pleads for the intervention of the Magistrate to make her husband give her enough for sustenance. While the jeering crowd and the indifferent husband remain insensitive to her pain and humiliation, the young second wife promises to care for her and tenderly leads her away. Corbett observes that it is one of the moments that made him aware of the dignity of the women of the Himalayan villages.

The novels under study are among the most articulate and detailed expressions of woman bonding that can be found in regional women writing in India. They examine the socio-cultural context that proves to be a crucible of sexism for women. The configurations of bonding recorded in them foreground the psychic osmosis among women. Woman bonding is projected as an ultimately enabling rather than inhibiting means to individual and collective transcendence to personhood. Thus we see an evolving paradigm that would historicize the psychoanalytic descriptions of subject formation.

The several astonishing similarities in the creative sensibilities of Ashapurna Devi and Sulekha Sanyal, manifested in their textual strategy, are definitely worth mentioning here. In their fiction, affiliations among women emerge as an important alternative plot displacing the man-woman relationship or the romantic love plot from the centre of the text. They study not autonomous and separate characters but relationships between characters. Both writers study female relationships in the wider context in which they take place: the emotional, political, economic, and symbolic structures of family and society. The similitude becomes more pronounced when they identify the woman who has become a subject as the instrument of social change.

Chapter IV

Initiatives from the Inner spaces

The crucial importance of the challenge raised by women writers like Ashapurna Devi and Sulekha Sanyal against a historiographical elision of women from the reform discourses in Bengal is yet to be acknowledged. Their novels are rearticulations of history. In their efforts to incorporate women into history, they first concern themselves with the exceptional women and then extend their enquiries into the majority of women unaccounted for by traditional historiography. They study the position of women in family and the family's position within the society to see how all human beings are turned into social creatures under the influence of the domestic order. Their work can rightly be called feminist analyses of history and demonstrates that the 'private' and 'public' are interdependent, with experience in each realm affecting the other. Thus they assert that the personal is political.

This chapter focuses, first on the initiatives of the protagonists of the novels analyzed in this study, and then on the reflections of their gestures in the lives of the women around them. These protagonists are secure in their faith in her-ethics, the ethics that speaks about one's obligation to the self and the species.

The history of the nineteenth century Bengal is a polyphonous sign in which differently stressed tonalities intersect. Significant rearticulations of social and cultural norms took place in the last decades of the century. The 'woman question' was central to the ameliorative projects because both the colonial government and the social reformers focused their attention on this particular aspect of the society, accepting the theory that the status of women was an indicator of the society's progress. Thus Hindu conjugality and domestic life became contested ground and the government and reformers took up sculpting a new woman as an important task.

But the urges behind the colonial government and the native reformers' ideological positioning were different. The profound symbolism embodied in the reformist ideology is worth probing because this symbolism pervades all the arrangements made by the powerful for the powerless. The underpinnings of imperial interests are visible in the government's attempts in fashioning the individual, especially the woman. Discussing the reformative schemes in the nineteenth century India (focused mainly in Bengal), Geraldine Forbes says: "The British regarded their domination of the subcontinent as proof of their moral superiority. In arguments over how to best rule their colonial subjects in India, they were led to discussions of the ideal relationship between men and women". (*Women in Modern India* 13). Jasodhara Bagchi is also unconvinced about the sincerity of the colonizer's interest in the woman question. She observes that India was one of the major conquests and most prized trophies of the 'enlightened' West.

> The 'Orient' was the tantalizing feminine, mysterious and dark or alternatively, a sleeping princess to be woken by the magic wand of the Occident as the Prince Charming. The Salvationist rhetoric of the missionaries joined hands with the emancipatory one of the colonizer to make Indian womanhood the emblem of the downtrodden society of the subcontinent. (*Indian Women: Myth and Reality* 3)

They were not very optimistic about a complete regeneration, but considered a new gender ideology as a necessary prelude to social change.

The male reformers of India also wished to reconfigure the patriarchal traditions and prescriptions of the past. Their reformist ideology was characterized by the colonial politics of masculinity and hegemony. Discussing the 'enlightened paternalism' subsumed within the reformist ideology of the time, Tanika Sarkar says:

> The home, then, had to substitute for the world outside and for all the work and relations there that lay beyond personal comprehension and control. . . . The *karta* [the head of the household], therefore, becomes within the home what he can never aspire to be outside it--a ruler, an administrator, a legislator or a chief justice, a general marshalling his troops. (*Hindu Wife, Hindu Nation* 38)

The true patriotic subject in this 'embryonic nation' (43) was the woman. But the cultural preoccupations and redefinitions of this period did not include women as partners in the schemes created for their regeneration. The ideologue of reform was problematised by many absences and voids—the absence of the woman's voice. The central issue was the status of women and ideally it should have developed into a dialogue between the reformer and the to-be-reformed. But even when the woman question loomed large and woman became the site on which tradition was debated and reformulated, her opinions were not sought or acknowledged. According to Geraldine Forbes, "This was not a question of 'what do women want?' but rather 'how can they be modernized?'" (*Women in Modern India* 12) Discussions were focused on what men wished for, not what women wanted as well. Discussing the rewriting of patriarchy in the late nineteenth century Bengal, Judith E. Walsh quotes Dhirendra Pal, an advice manual writer, who argued that women's education was essential to a companionate marriage but it was to be a special and separate kind. In the introduction to his text, *Strir Sahit Kathopakathan*, [Conversations with the Wife], he says:

> Women folk have one task in this world, men another. So there is no possibility that a single type of education for both will produce anything but harm . . . so women should be educated in all those things which are essential for a woman when she lives in a family, all that would make her a learned and cultured woman, a woman who is devoted to *dharma* and one who is worthy to be called a true wife. (qtd. *What Women Learned* 656)

While discussing the reform projects in Kerala, J. Devika remembers that the Sanskrit scholar Punnassery Nambi had believed in a female education which was confined to learning letters and basic arithmetic that would help women to be skillful housewives. He recommended a scheme that would be helpful in preparing Antarjanams for performance of daily rituals and practices carried out in *illams* and the essentials of kitchen management. It was further recommended that Antarjanams may be given adequate knowledge of Sanskrit, not for the attainment of a cultured mind but for avoiding mistakes in chanting *stottrams.* (*Engendering Individuals* 152)

The surprising similarity in the thoughts of Dhirendra Pal and Punnassery Nambi reveals the ill-concealed reluctance of new patriarchy to accept woman as an autonomous subject. Her life was still expected to be organized around conjugality and rituals.

The reformist movement was further problematised by the consistent, stereotyped portrayal of the upper caste woman as ever-silent victims. J. Devika's observation on *Namboothiri* reformism in Kerala echoes Geraldine Forbes' views about the reform movement in colonial Bengal. Forbes argues that reformers believed that women were first to be pitied and then reformed. Devika concludes that in Kerala also, "One of the issues that received considerable attention in reformist literature and theatre was the 'condition of Antarjanams', and they were set up, again and again as victims who needed to be 'led' out of their plight, as if passivity were a necessary attribute of the oppressed" (128). It was as though one could not think of reforming the Antarjanam without first projecting her as a helpless victim.

Women were thus treated as an undifferentiated, homogenized mass of victims. There were harbingers of rebellion from among the collective of women but they were overshadowed by the Reformer-Man. K. Saradamoni challenges the attempt to reduce the whole complex enterprise of reformism to a male effort and says that women were by this time becoming aware of the deprivations in their life. In *Matriliny Transformed,* she observes that in Kerala women were arguing effectively that they should have access to the same fund of knowledge as men.

> They answered the criticisms that education would take away from women their feminine qualities and attachment to and care for the home. Padmavati Amma, a strong supporter of women's education was against confusing 'fashion' with progress. She wanted refinement in thought and deeds. Another writer Kavamma firmly stated that English had become a world language and that western education had become part of Kerala life. (119)

The presence of such women in the movement was a challenge flung at tradition and initiated a search for alternative strategies for social improvement, but the curious process of decentering kept them effectively out of history.

This decentering is challenged by Ashapurna Devi and Sulekha Sanyal. They give language to the intra-subjective and corporeal experiences left mute by culture in the past.

While discussing Isak Dineson's short story, 'The Blank Page' as a metaphor for two major concerns of feminist scholarship, deconstructing dominant male patterns of thought and reconstructing previously ignored female experience, Gayle Greene and Coppelia Kahn argue:

> History has been a record of male experience, written by men, from a male perspective. What has been designated historically significant has been deemed so according to a valuation of power and activity in the public world. . . . It is the task of historians of women to reconstruct the female experience, the buried and neglected past, to fill in the blank pages and make the silences speak. (*Making a Difference* 12, 13).

The novels under this study reconstruct female experiences and breathe life into a buried past. In them, female voices are keenly listened to and recorded. Dialogic relationships among women are acknowledged and herethics, as an ideology, is celebrated. The dynamics of the domestic space is projected as the impetus behind the many and far-reaching socio-cultural changes. In her preface to *Pratham Pratishruti* Ashapurna Devi says:

> The history of times past is made up of stories about the rise and fall of the public world. And that restless, clamorous history writ against a backdrop of light and darkness holds out inspiration, ardour and excitement for the future. But is not the mute domestic space similarly broken and built? From which flows forth the changing colours of a community, an age, and people's mentalities? We would find abundant treasures if only we focused there. But history has invariably overlooked the dynamics of the domestic world. That domain has always been neglected. This book is about an unknown woman who was among those who carved out the etchings of a promise from within those ignored interior spaces of Bengal.

In their fiction, Ashapurna Devi, and Sulekha Sanyal critique a tradition that makes victims of women. The oppressiveness of the system is effectively and powerfully portrayed but resistance is placed side by side. The lives within the traditional brahmin household, with all its stifling inhuman customs, are reconstructed, but at the same time, females who strive for personhood, who display signs of being individuals, and their strategies to resist tradition are also recreated. They assert that women's status is not monolithic and static. The premium is placed upon the individual's ability to relate to her collective, to establish amicable relations. The importance of such relationships in bringing about change is put forth effectively. The presence of the male reformer is not completely denied as Bhavathosh master in *Pratham Pratishruti*, Ambika Kumar in *Subarnalatha*, and Adhir in *Nabankur* prove, but the focus is on the female reformers.

Pratham Pratishruti is an effective discourse on the initiatives that stir in the inner spaces and move in concentric circles to the outer spaces. The confluence of physical, emotional, intellectual and social characteristics of a human being mark Satyabati, the protagonist of *Pratham Pratishruti,* as a person. She stands, like the proud Eve of Kabita Sinha's poem *Eswar ke Eve* [Eve Speaks to God] who asserts that she was the first to break the shackles and that she was the first rebellion on earth, as the first in a tradition of awakened women who dares to transcend the inviolate and inviolable boundaries to reach personhood.

Satyabati has all the qualities that define a reformer—the instinctive understanding of absences or shortcomings that can cripple life, the courage to demand and fight for rights and a moral sensibility which includes the collective in its thoughts. Hence her transgressions reach out of the private domain to make impact on the public domain. Her life invests the word pioneer with total meaning because she is a thinking person born into an age of unthinking masses and a moral being born into a corrupt society. All the different aspects of the woman's question, education, seclusion, economic independence and conjugality are subjected to her thoughts and consideration and strengthen her personhood. Her transgressions relate directly or indirectly to each of them. Each single gain feeds in to the gains of the collective.

Satyabati's transgressions are of two kinds: some of them are keenly felt within personal and familial realms while others create serious ruptures that are noticed by the society. Satya locates the reason for the inferior status and lack of agency of women in her society in ignorance and identifies the denial of the right to education as gross injustice. So she begins her transgressions by fighting for the right to education. Her responses to criticism, varying from playfully ironical to furiously argumentative emphasize her faith in the potentially transforming power of education.

The patriarchal male's antagonism to women's education is rooted in his anxieties about the potential danger of sexual intrigues, since a literate woman can write and make secret, illicit assignations. In Satya's case, such anxieties prove to be baseless but she raises a more powerful challenge to the ideology of male hegemony by using her hard-won privilege, literacy, as a tool for protest. The nine-year-old Satya makes up rhymes about the village bully, Jatadharan, who beats his wife till she becomes unconscious, and with her gang of playmates, roams the village chanting them.

> The Elephant-footed Jata da—there he goes the blighter! May a toad kick the back of this stupid wife-beater! Jata, Jata's really gross, he's an abuser like no other! Watch the fun, for now he'll run, here comes the wife's father! (*First Promise* 31)

Thus she stages the first-ever protest against domestic violence witnessed by the village. The strategy of using literacy as a tool for protest reaches its culmination when Satya, now in her thirties, writes a severely-worded letter of complaint to the colonial government, demanding their intervention in the murder case of Puti, a nine-year old child bride murdered by her husband for refusing his conjugal rights. When the white Sahib policeman comes, she makes a spirited appeal for justice.

> There are heaps of sins that have collected over centuries. If you can rid us of those, only then would I say that you deserve to be lawmakers. Why have you taken on the guise of a ruler in another's land? Why can't you just huddle in to your ships and leave? (484)

Satya's critique of social injustices and administrative lapses are informed by a moral sensibility trained by reading and observation.

Education also opens avenues for interactive, meaningful friendships. Satya turns an informal gathering of women at *Sarvamangalatala* Temple into a class. Teaching has always been her passion and an intensely pleasurable experience, but her role as a teacher in *Sarvamangala Vidyalaya* has a fuller meaning. Her eagerness and the reciprocative enthusiasm of her students, all middle-aged housewives, create an environment conducive to attitudinal changes. She describes her teaching experience thus: "Except for one or two, they are learning fast. If you saw them you would realize how eager they are to read the *Puranas* and the epics. It's so satisfying to see that." (394). She is excited by the courage and the initiative exhibited by her students in going to the *Brahmo* leader, Keshubchandra Sen's house to witness the historic meeting between him and Paramahamsa. By this they reject two brahminical norms at one stroke—they challenge caste by visiting a *brahmo*'s house and gender by travelling without male company. As a woman who has attained personhood, it is infinitely satisfying for Satyabati to watch other women taking their first steps towards the same goal and her words describing their journey reflect her pleasure. "So many women went. We went in a group--hired a horse-coach and shared the cost--the greater the number, the more the strength! What wonderful singing! so soothing!" (395). Thus the mute women of the antahpuram transform themselves into an eloquent community of dolphins through the agency of a woman, without male interventions.

Economic independence and education are complementary, intersecting areas of thought and in Satya's case education is the direct cause of economic empowerment. Her decision to sell her bangles to pay the white sahib doctor to treat Nabakumar and to give her gold chain as a gift to a boy in Calcutta are gestures that mark non-compliance. In the Bengali brahmin family of her time, the money and jewellery given to the woman by her natal family as gifts become the property of the conjugal family and the bride is only a mannequin to display them. But Satya refuses to be a mannequin. Her final rejection of patrimony is also an act of non-compliance and a more important one because when she rejects the landholdings given by her father, in effect she refuses to accept the charity of any male. It is an eloquent testimony to the courage of a woman who has conquered the fears and insecurities about a woman's capacity to face life alone. The last words spoken by her in the novel underscore her assertion of economic independence. "A long time ago, before Subarna was born, I'd opened a school and would play at teaching women—do you remember that? I will find out if I still remember that game. It should earn a woman enough for her keep." (534) This seemingly individual gesture initiates profound social and familial changes affecting the subject-object equation in male-female relationships.

Satyabati's gestures of resistance and non-compliance make serious ruptures with the dominant system. Her battles against the orthodox society of *kulin* brahmins create tremendous ripples in the stagnant little village of *Baruipur* (her affinal village) and the ripples gradually grow into tidal waves of change. She challenges the infallibility of the indigenous medical system and ushers in the system of modern medicine. This decentering of *Ayurveda*, traditional system of medicine, has another important consequence. A white doctor enters the inner quarters of an upper caste Hindu household and an upper caste Hindu takes the medicines touched by a *mleccha* and thus caste itself becomes a contested ground. Satya keeps on challenging caste by coming to Calcutta and by drinking tap water and problematises the issue further by learning English. Thus the axiomatic brahminical prescriptions about caste purity receive a serious challenge from a woman.

Satya's friendship with Bhavathosh Master redefines male-female relationships and defies the norms of seclusion, which travesties the integrity of a woman. Traditionally, a woman's relationships with the opposite sex are restricted to the male members of her family. Here a woman introduces a tremendous change by proving that she can have a perfectly normal relationship with a male outside kinship relations. It adds new dimensions to the conventional interpretations of male-female relationship and marks the beginnings of healthy friendships built on mutual respect, uncoloured by love or lust.

Satya violates the timeless tradition of all the members of a family living together. For the first time in the history of Baruipur, a woman steps out of the patriarchal, Hindu undivided family and establishes a smaller unit where husband, wife and children live without the in-laws or other elders to supervise. Thus the large extended family gives way to the closely-knit small family. It is crucially important that this moving out does not signify a total breaking up with the family and the collective. Satya comes back to her affinal family whenever her presence is needed there and maintains close contacts with Saudamini, her sister-in-law. She thus effectively asserts her right to be an independent subject without severing the ties with the collective and successfully claims her right to mobility that was earlier denied to women.

Thus Satya becomes the instrument of an important social change. But it is not merely the beginning of the end of the joint family system. It marks the beginning of a change in the very way of living in the rural areas. The rural way of living is replaced by the urban. Young, educated men like Nabakumar realize that living off the land is an outdated aspiration and seek jobs elsewhere away from their native villages, leaving the land behind. Earlier, the rural families depended solely on agricultural income even when the land holdings and the income from it were inadequate to feed all in a large extended family. The breaking up of the joint family and the awareness about the job opportunities available for the educated in the public and private sectors pave the way for a socio-economic revolution.

The greatest act of defiance Satya hurls at the society is the final renunciation. When she leaves her family, she redefines Hindu conjugality. The *shastras* dictate that Hindu marriages are sacrosanct and hence eternal. But as already discussed in Chapter I, *smritis* are interpreted with strong gender biases and they invariably prove detrimental to the female. Cruelty, unfaithfulness, broken promises and moral and physical coercions are not sufficient reasons for the female to repudiate her role as a wife. Satya, by alienating herself from her husband, puts the ideology of conjugality into searing question. She leaves with questions that generations of women will continue to ask: "Do the gods really come and bless every marriage? Are all marriage bonds for this life and beyond? Those are the things I want to ask." (531)

Significantly, she does not wait for the male world's intervention in re-articulating the cultural and religious prescriptions. She does not wait for the male reformer to rescue her, but takes the important decision that transforms her life and the life of her immediate society.

The responses of three women, who associate with Satya with varying degrees of closeness, to her transgressions illustrate how one woman can influence her collective and thereby initiate social changes. Saudamini, Satya's sister-in-law and ally from the first day of her life in the affinal family, is deeply influenced by Satya. At the difficult moments when Satya's perceptions, which differ radically from that of others, make her the object of hot criticism or chilling ridicule, Sadu sees into the rationality and truth of her arguments and offers her support. Two such occasions are specifically important because on both occasions Sadu's reactions eloquently prove how even a very ordinary woman is awakening to the plight of women, and is thinking about the ways to assert her personhood. On the first occasion when Satya's interpretation of illiteracy as blindness invites scathing sarcasm from all, Sadu refuses to join them and looks back into her meaningless yester years through the eyes of Satya. She says: "I don't think she is wrong, Naba. Had I learning enough to write a letter, I need not have wasted my life away" (502).

The second occasion is more crucial because here Satya leaves conjugality and seals her fate off as an outcaste. From now on, her name will be taboo among *kulin* brahmins. Still Sadu dares to support her and to leave Baruipur with her. The palpable anger and hostility of others fail to frighten her. She is now capable of seeing through the worthless martyr act of the guilty male and watches Nabakumar with ill-concealed derision. Thus Sadu starts using her mental faculties, thinks her own thoughts and becomes a part of the decision-making process.

One of the prominent examples of woman bonding in the novel, of one woman positioning herself as a subject and then inspiring others to transcend their limitations, can be seen in the relationship between Satya and Suhasini. Suhasini, the orphaned girl moulded by Satya to her heart's desire, shares all her enthusiasm for books and learning and her idealism. When she transcends the lowly, limiting circumstances of her birth and steers the course of her life as a subject, Satya's project of sculpting the new woman is materialized without external interventions.

But the impact of Satya's forceful personality and her reformative zeal can be best appreciated when sparks of understanding dawn even in Bhabini's mind which is dense with ignorance and jealousy. Bhabini is one of the many village women who enjoy the fruits of Satya's initiatives which enable them (after Satya has set up the example) to come out of the stifling inner spaces of the joint family to the comparatively freer environment of the nuclear family in Calcutta. But she does not try to understand Satya and is jealous of the respect she wins from different quarters. She is aware of Satya's competence and her own inadequacies shame her. So she finds solace and joy in criticizing Satya. But her little sister Puti's death awakens her to the injustices imposed on women in the name of male marital rights. Even though like the others in her family, she believes that it is the girl's fate and hence resolves not to fight against it, for the first time she approves of Satya's difference and congratulates her. She says:

> I think it is a good idea that nowadays they wait for girls to get a little older before marrying them off. A good thing too that you have started sending Subarna to school. It will increase her understanding and her strength. (477)

The very fact that a woman like Bhabini is capable of applying her mind to issues like child marriage and the advantages of women's education is symptomatic of the changes that are in store. The change in Bhabini is sporadic and inconsistent while in Saudamini it is deeper. In Suhasini, it is consistent and all-pervading and effects transcendence and transformation. Together these three women represent the community of women around Satyabati waking up from their lethargic existence and mark the slow and painful journey towards personhood.

Subarna, the protagonist of *Subarnalatha* is, in Julia Kristeva's terms, a subject-in-process. She lives and functions with in the symbolic order which is regulated by the male. Her position is marginal and tenuous because she is positioned as an object of desire, not as a subject who desires. But she refuses to be an object forever, asserts her identity as a subject and even as she participates in the existing order, strives for the creation of a different one. Her life is more stifling than that of her mother, Satyabati, and so her transgressions are mostly confined to the domestic space, but they shake the foundation of her affinal home and the tremors move centrifugally to affect the immediate society.

Subarna is criticized and ridiculed from the very beginning because she is the daughter of a woman who has committed the unpardonable sin of repudiating conjugality, but the orthodox conjugal family fails to kill her spirit. She manages to force open a few windows to usher the wind of change into the musty rooms that smell of decadence. Thus the changing socio-political ideologies make their belated but inevitable presence felt within the hard-core traditionalism of the family. This is manifested in the change that comes over Prabhas Chandran, Subarna's extremely orthodox and chauvinistic brother-in-law, and her sons in their attitude to nationalism, patriotism and women's education.

Most women of the nineteenth century Bengal had internalized the norms which describe femaleness as a sin and experienced the shame and guilt associated with it. But Satyabati, Subarna's mother, had never been ashamed of her femaleness and thus never passed on any negative notions about the body to her daughter. Naturally Subarna never considers her body as unclean or as a source of shame. She challenges the irony and callousness of cherishing the healthy female body as an object of pleasure and ignoring it completely when it is racked with pain during childbirth. She is furious when her husband refers to child-birth as 'women's business' and when her mother-in-law treats it as an unmentionable subject.

In Subarna's affinal home, as in all average Bengali households of the time, child-birth is unmentionable outside the closed female space. The Bengali woman does not go to the extent to which her Victorian English counterpart would go to spare her husband the anxieties related to the birthing process. In *Of Woman Born*, Adrienne Rich quotes from a volume of letters written by the wives of manual labourers and published by the Women's Co-operative Guild in Britain in 1915 to show how these letters speak about the common belief that women should spare their men, who had worked hard all day, from further strain at home. One woman, in her letter says:

> I dare not let my husband in his precarious condition hear a cry of pain from me, and travail pain can not always be stifled; and here again the doctor helped me by giving me a sleeping draught to administer him as soon as I felt the pangs of child-birth. Hence he slept in one room while I travailed in the other and brought forth the liveliest boy that ever gladdened a mother's heart. (51)

The location of the posterior female space of a Bengali household makes the sleeping draught unnecessary, but still the smallest, darkest and dirtiest room within the inner quarters is used as the birthing chamber and the woman is admonished not to utter a single cry. Subarna is furious with the system which glorifies motherhood and remains indifferent to the pain of mothering and the health of the mother. She insists on using clean beds and bedsheets in the birthing room and an irate Muktakeshi has, at last, to succumb to her demands. Thus one of the most important battles Subarna fights is to establish the worth of the female body and to state that it is not merely an object on which the male can satisfy himself.

Subarna's transgressions are symptomatic of a deeply ingrained faith in and urge for personhood and obviously they are not confined to thoughts about the body. The socio-economic compulsions that initiate and hasten the migration of the village people to the cities during Satya's time are non-existent in Subarna's case. Still she insists on setting up a house of her own within walkable distance from the affinal home because she is driven by an urge to create a space of her own where she can be alone. Ashapurna Devi describes her psycho-dynamics thus:

> Subarna stood on the roof, under the dark sky, staring at its glittering stars. For this, at least, she was grateful. In her new house, she could escape from all eyes and all questions. Even if it was only for a short while, she could forget how tightly bound she was to her role as wife and mother. Away from the business of running a busy household, she could seek a few moments of peace, and just be herself. (*Subarnalatha*139)

To Subarna, claiming the space is synonymous with the craving for self-expression and it becomes central to her very existence. The anonymity imposed on woman by conjugality and the urge to transcend the confining anonymity are major concerns in her *Smritikatha.* In the introduction to *Subarnalatha*, the translator Gopa Majumdar says:

> Subarnalatha is painfully aware of her lack of identity as an individual. The anonymity of a woman comes out quite

> strongly in connection with the book she writes . . . her dream is—"the first page of her printed book would bear her name, 'Sreemati Subarnalata Devi.'" And in her book she writes—"I am a housewife. My only name is Mejobou. I have a mind, a soul, but no one acknowledges my existence." (xii)

But *Smritikatha* is not merely an emotional outpouring of personal anguish. The book dwells on intersecting thoughts about women, autonomy, nation, community and freedom. With intuitive understanding, she focuses on the fate of thousands of women in Bengal and sympathizes with the women who are unaware of the emptiness of their existence. She looks hopefully into the future and envisages the new, awakened woman who with flashing eyes and firm voice will point her finger at the male and say:

> Our curse will befall you. You won't be able to keep us blind forever. The dictum that the husband is the woman's lord and master will be obliterated. You will have to do penance. Your cruelty and meanness will not be forgiven. (182)

Smritikatha symbolizes multiple repudiations which are strongly resonant of her mother's defiant gestures and speaks of a sensibility far ahead of its time. Subarna portrays a life that has been starved of love and made to stagnate in the inner quarters. More importantly she refuses to be the looking glass that flatters the male ego and convince him that he is, by nature, superior to half the human race. In *A Room of One's Own*, Virginia Woolf says: "Women have served all these centuries as looking glasses possessing the magic and delicious power of reflecting the figure of man at twice its natural size" (41). But Subarna is neither a flatterer nor one to be flattered because, as a wife and as a writer, she is honest and will not trade her soul for peace. She considers her marriage a profound deception and does not resort to lies when she describes her relationship with her husband.

> "I hate my husband." said the young Subarna [in *Smritikatha*] "I tried to love him, I trusted him completely when he told me he would take me see my father. I did everything he asked me to do . . . disgusting ghastly things that made me sick. But, in the end, he went back on his word and laughed in my face. I know he will come back to me and profess undying love, just to get what he wants. I also know it is my duty to be obedient and to love him in return. But—help me God—this is one duty I can not fulfill. I can not make myself love a man whose mind is as ugly as his face is handsome." (182, 183)

She also remembers how her poetic, romantic self was ruthlessly killed by the physicality of his approach.

> 'We've had enough poetry for one night', he proclaimed, 'As it is, you are never interested in your duties, are you? Come now, I have other plans. . . .' He blew hard on the flickering lamp, making it go out at once. But was it just the room that was plunged in darkness? Didn't Subarna's whole future get engulfed by it? (185)

Smritikatha thus anticipates a modern woman writer who can speak about herself and her relationships without guilt and shame. In a powerful move, Ashapurna Devi makes the woman writer speak, with rare courage, as the subject without waiting for the male writers to write about her as a passive object of oppression. Women writers of many years to come are thus present in Subarna's self and text.

Subarna's transgressions are continued by two of her daughters, Bakul and Parul, who are as intensely involved in the process of subjectification as their mother was. Overtly, Parul remains outside the orbit of Subarna's influence because the dissimilarities between them are many and varied. Emotional outbursts are alien to Parul's nature and unlike Subarna, she will not waste her energy by knocking at the doors of the deaf world. She is capable of withdrawing into an ironic silence and active inner life. But the fiercely independent, fearless self of Subarna is reborn in her. When the middle-aged, widowed Parul chooses to live alone in a house on the banks of the Ganga, turning down the invitations of her married sons, she defies the age-old custom that the mother should be controlled and protected by her grown-up sons. She ignores the snide remarks of her neighbours who express their displeasure at a woman who ignores her duties as a mother and grandmother and establishes her right to live as she pleases. Thus the trajectories of Subarna and Parul's lives, with their respective craving for the red-tiled open verandah and the lonely majesty of the shores of the Ganga, mark two stages in the female's voyage to personhood.

Reconfiguration of patriarchal spaces is one of the thematic concerns of *Bakulkatha*, the third novel in the trilogy. The physical positioning and the architectural features of the inner quarters had conspired with gendered division of labour to make the concept and practice of seclusion inviolable. The ideology of exclusion functioned within the ideas of domesticity and seclusion because the female was effectively excluded from the activities of the mind and intellect. Bakul, the protagonist of *Bakulkatha*, challenges the concepts of seclusion and exclusion. She symbolizes a woman's near absolute control over her space in the material and metaphorical sense of the term. Her rooms transform themselves into the posterior area in the large house because she refuses to be shut in. As one of the most successful writers of her time, her presence is eagerly sought and her words are avidly listened to and thus the world includes her. At the same time, the members of her society, the intelligentsia and the illiterate, male and female, the rich and the poor—come to see her and talk to her and thus the world aspires to be included in her space. This mutuality of inclusion enables Bakul to assert her personhood while helping her collective to assert theirs.

Operations of power, symbolized by the strategies of exclusion and inclusion can be seen in Bakul's relationship with her family also. She is capable of excluding others if and when she decides and never allows the family to impose their authority on her. The overtly reticent, soft-spoken Bakul is endowed with a quiet strength which can keep prying eyes and probing hands away from her space. Her rooms are her private domain and her brothers, even though they are resentful of her freedom, do not dare to violate her privacy. Thus Bakul asserts her right to privacy which has been denied to the women of the earlier generations. Her mother Subarnalatha had never had a room of her own and her yearning for an open verandah had once scandalized her family. A dark, ill-ventilated room and the staircase to the terrace that was never built speak about the physical space denied to her. She transcended these limitations by never surrendering her inner space to any one. In the next generation, Bakul establishes her authority over external and internal spaces and thus marks one more stage in the woman's journey.

Bakul's Calcutta, Bengal in general, is different from Subarna's in terms of women's education and freedom. The number of educated and working women is indicative of the efforts of pioneering women like Satyabati and Subarna coming to fruition. But still there are factions in the society that remain suspicious of women's attempts to redefine themselves and are anxious about the influence an awakened woman can exert on her collective. Bakul's brother Manu and his wife Ramla are worried about their daughter Shampa's love for Bakul. As mentioned in Chapter III, Bakul and Shampa, the aunt and niece, share a very deep and loving bond and Bakul's presence is strongly felt in Shampa's life. Defiant daughters are not welcome in her parents' narrow-minded existence and they blame Bakul for

Shampa's transgressions locating their source in Bakul's support.

In the painful days after Shampa's unconventional love and marriage, Ramla recognizes the ugly truth about misconceptions rooted in jealousy. She confesses to Bakul that she had always been jealous of her difference and her privileged space in the hearts of young girls like Shampa and that anger had made her blind. She says: "I am rightly punished, Bakul. Because of my anger and jealousy to you, I never loved my daughter enough. Never tried to understand her." (*Bakulinte Katha* 209, my translation). Thus an unawakened woman takes the first step to awakening through the agency of another, already awakened woman, and thereby develops a state of mind which enables her to acknowledge the validity of the perspectives of others. When Ramla accepts her daughter as an autonomous being and decides to let her steer the course of her life, the Hindu marriage system in which the girl is a volitionless object undergoes a change. Fifty years after the death of Muktakeshi, Shampa's great grandmother, three women—Bakul, Ramla and Shampa—transform her once orthodox household into a stage for an extremely significant social change. Muktakeshi's house witnesses the obliteration of class, caste distinctions and marriage of convenience giving way to marriage of love.

The narrative movement in *Nabankur: The Seedling's Tale* marks a troubled phase in the social and political history of Bengal. The protagonist, Chhobi, lives in a time characterized by anti-colonial agitations, the advent of the Second World War and the infamous Bengal Famine. Sulekha Sanyal situates her on the very edge of a tidal shift that introduces the upper caste, *kulin* brahmin women to many unfamiliar alternatives.

There are many commonalities between Chhobi and the female protagonists of Ashapurna Devi's trilogy, Satyabati,

Subarna and Bakul. Like them she is driven by an inner urge to attain personhood. The novel opens with Chhobi opening her eyes to the light of a new day and the images of light and vision become the central signifiers in the text. Her perceptions are, just as Satya, Subarna and Bakul are in the trilogy, crucial to the story and they help her define her sense of self and at the same time mark her as a part of her collective. The conflict is between what Chhobi is as a person and what conventional definitions of womanhood require her to be.

In the introduction to *Nabankur*, Himani Bannerjee says: "From the outset she is presented as being different, as odd and special or precious, from others of her age—both boys and girls" (xiv). Her difference is rooted in her resistance against the society's attempt to bend her into a sexed form. Unlike the other girls of her age, she does not care for fairy tales or dolls and enters on a serious quest for her self. She feels that a sharp, insistent voice is asking the questions—Who is she? What is she?—from deep within. Patriarchy has certain conventional answers for such questions but Chhobi is not satisfied with them. Her family and society tell her that she is just a female, not a boy, not even a human being, just a girl. As a girl, she is not supposed to talk loudly, laugh or read. There can be no hope and ambition for girls. Chhobi, like Satya and Subarna, refuses to accept this answer and is determined to search for true meanings.

But there are certain political and social factors that intervene in Chhobi's journey towards personhood and make her transgressions different from the others. Chhobi's Bengal is situated in a time span between those of Subarna and Bakul and the weakening of the absolute power of Brahmanism is one of the crucial changes that have come over the societal profile. This mitigation of the brahminical, patriarchal power does not mean a complete emancipation for women and the woman issue is not yet resolved. Even though Chhobi's grandfather and grandmother represent old patriarchy and try to prevent the girl's attempts to individuate through moral and physical coercion, her problems are different from those of Satya and Subarna. Child marriage and the ban on literacy are no longer issues that are to be addressed urgently. What problematises Chhobi's life is the subtle shift of power from old patriarchy to new patriarchy which is imaged through the fall of Dakshinaranjan Ray, her grandfather, and the ascendance to power of Kuladaranjan, her father.

New patriarchy, represented by Kuladaranjan Ray, believes, like old patriarchy, that ultimately a woman's future lies in marriage. But it also believes that a peripheral knowledge of letters and numbers will add to the value of the girl. Thus one year of elementary education is now not denied. But aspirations for higher education, which can lead to subjectification, are actively discouraged. Kuladaranjan's response to the news of Chhobi's matriculation results shows that the difference between old patriarchy and new patriarchy are minimal and that their attitude to women has not undergone change in any substantive sense. Old patriarchy had once refused Chhobi the same share of food the boys get and now new patriarchy trivializes her achievement because she is only a girl. Kuladaranjan enthusiastically congratulates his nephew Poltu even though his marks are not as good as Chhobi's. He says, "Poltu, it is you who will keep the flag flying. It is you who have understood my struggles. The rest of them, well" (*Nabankur* 242).

Kuladaranjan's anxieties about the impact of higher education on girls prove true because Chhobi aspires for emancipation at multiple levels. She equates, like Satya and Subarna, the freedom of the individual with the freedom of the country and further equates the freedom of the country with that of the downtrodden. Even as a young girl she agonizes over the invisibility thrust upon the poor, the low caste and women. The eight-year-old Chhobi watches her grandfather beating Shashi Majhi, the fisherman, and in her eyes, he has lost all his moral right to make her obey him. She says: "Dadu is so horrid and cruel. He beat Shashi Majhi for no reason at all! Why should you go, just because he's called you?" (19) Thus sympathy for the poor and aversion to autocracy become the twin intersecting cores that inform Chhobi's political alertness and moral sensibility. Her ability to sympathize with the suffering poor is manifested in her friendship with Nilu and Pilu, daughters of her aunt's poor neighbour, and Paribanu a muslim girl who toils to raise money for her schooling.

When the sixteen-year-old educated Chhobi comes back to the village from her aunt's house in town, her sympathy has deepened into empathy. The ghastly spectacle of hunger in the famine-stricken village, of skeletal arms holding out pots for some gruel, disturbs her so much that she openly defies the prescriptions of gender, caste and class. For the first time a *kulin* brahmin girl gets involved in the peasant movement which is gaining momentum in the village. She prefers activism to ideology and marches along with the low caste villagers to the SDO's office to demand a relief kitchen and joins them in their protests against the black-marketeering landlords who are her own people. She works in the relief kitchen, cooking food and distributing it among the poor, and thus becomes the first respectable woman to mingle with what her grandfather calls "riff raff".

Chhobi thus breaks many social taboos and inaugurates a new era where the boundaries of class and caste disintegrate. A new socio-political environment which holds the upper class responsible and answerable for the injustices heaped on the downtrodden comes into being through the initiative of a woman. This disintegration of the feudal, brahminical system is symbolized in the novel by the weakening of the power of the Rays. The defiant daughter of the family gives them the message, in no uncertain terms, that the concepts of the infallibility and moral authority of the brahmin will not survive in the blazing anger of the hungry, marginalized masses.

Chhobi's acts of non-compliance are sharp and deal terrible blows to the male ego. She is a reflective person by nature and the confluence of her experiences and reflections convinces her that compromises pose the gravest threat to personhood. All around her, she sees women who are forced to accept the accommodating postures of femininity. Patriarchy demands implicit obedience from the females and the woman's compliance protects the male ego from getting wounded. Chhobi is not prepared to be compliant and diplomacy is not one among her many attributes and thus the sensitive balance between male pride and female servility is overturned. She refuses to present herself before the prospective bridegroom chosen for her. Chhobi believes that as a person she has complete authority over herself and hence is not prepared to be an object that can be transferred from the ownership of one male to another. She is determined to put an end to the system which is indifferent to the girl's feelings.

Chhobi, thus, subverts the familiar, gendered codes which protect the male ego from mortifications while denying the same right to the female. Dakshinaranjan Ray is forced to apologise with folded hands before the prospective bridegroom's father and present Sephu, another granddaughter, instead of Chhobi, and for the first time realizes how infinitely painful humiliation is. (Incidentally, Chhobi's defiance reminds us of Indulekha, the bold protagonist of Chandu Menon's novel of the same title, who deals a painful blow to the ego of Soori Namboothiripad, the rich, foolish brahmin who comes to her house to begin *sambandham*.) Chhobi's transgression is important because it is not motivated by narrow self-interest. When she interrogates patriarchy's right to treat a woman as a servile object characterized by humility and obedience, she has the greater interests of her collective at heart. She is beaten, bruised and shut up in a dark room but does not wallow in self-pity. Her thoughts are centered on the changes her disobedience will bring about in the family and society. "She hoped no one in the house would ever be locked up in a room in such a way. Chhobi knew she was the last victim and took some consolation in the thought. Never in the future would such a thing happen again." (226)

Chhobi's refusal to participate in brahminical gender, caste and class proprieties problematises her life initially, but ultimately, like the other pioneering women, she is able to engage in constant contentions with the system and to bring in changes. When she leaves home the second time to go to Calcutta to join college, she normalizes the routine of leaving and returning which, hitherto, is a male privilege denied to girls. She further establishes the girl's right to aspire for higher, better destinies than marriage.

The success of Chhobi's initiatives can be best read in the responses of Shaila, a low caste, peasant girl and beneficiary of the relief kitchen and Saraswati, Chhobi's aunt. Shaila, and the other low caste children are half-dead with hunger during the days of the famine. The stoves in their houses stay cold and they live on the meagre food doled out to them in the relief kitchen. Chhobi teaches Shaila the alphabet and the little girl forgets the pangs of hunger, revelling in her newly attained skill.

> Shaila, having recently learnt to write her name, was writing it all over the place, often forgetting to eat. She would examine her own handiwork like a little child and say, 'Didi, I will teach every one. When these hard times are over, I am going

> to return to our village and open a school. I will be the teacher in that school. What do you think? (201)

Chhobi thus initiates a low-caste, economically disadvantaged girl to the world of letters and inspires her to dream about a better tomorrow. Together they teach the community to dream and to translate dreams in to realities.

Saraswati, Chhobi's kakima (paternal uncle's wife), is the representative of the mute inmates of the Ray household. She, like the other women of her time, feels guilty about being a woman and her consternation is intensified when she senses the silent accusations about her large brood of children eating into the dwindling resources of the family. But she never dares to point out the injustice of calling her the source of all trouble. She is the typical, silently suffering victim. Chhobi's presence and her transgressions motivate Saraswati's thought processes to come alive and her sensibility undergoes a great transformation. She becomes proud of femaleness. At a time when a girl child is least welcome in the house (due to the transgressions of Chhobi), Saraswati dares to be happy about being the mother of yet another daughter. She says that she would have liked Chhobi to hold the baby first. A deep bonding and consequent change surface when she looks deep into Chhobi's eyes and says: "Chhobu, I hope she takes after you" (233).

Shaila and Saraswati are important in the scheme of the novel, because they validate the truth about women's initiatives. They belong to two extremely different strata of the power structure of the society and project forth the ripples of change that are pervading the different levels. When they awaken to the possibilities of life and shake off the guilt and shame crystallized in their beings, society itself undergoes comprehensive changes.

The authors of these narratives and their characters are strong women who never allow compromises to lessen their quality as persons and who use their status as subjects to create more subjects out of the generations of women. Unlike the woman narrator in Sylvia Plath's poem, "Stings," who declares, "I am no drudge" and then anxiously asks "Will they hate me these women who only scurry, / Whose only news is the open cherry, the open clover?" (28-30) they confidently assert their personhood and then inspire the women farthest from awakening to follow their initiatives.

A crucial attitudinal difference between Plath and the two Indian women writers whose works are analysed here is also worth-examining. To Sylvia Plath, personhood is singularity and so it signals alienation from the community. But to our writers, it is a metaphor of positivism which signifies linkage between the individual and the collective. They situate their characters in a dialectic between autonomy and community and foreground the importance of affiliations even as they accept the differences. Their protagonists take up their positions as subjects in the existing order and then strive to create a new one. Thus they become harbingers of socio-cultural changes.

Importantly, this textual strategy of emphasizing the primacy of affiliations over singularity paves the way for a phenomenological interrelation among the authors, characters and readers. Discussing the evolving trends and techniques in the tradition of women's writing, Michelle Boulous Walker observes:

> The relationship between characters, between the author and her characters, between the author and her reader are all encoded as textual strategies which aim to deconstruct the logic of patriarchal discourse. The sharp distinction between autonomous and distant characters is replaced with a writing that stresses affiliation, interrelation and community. (*Philosophy and the Maternal Body* 160)

In the novels of Ashapurna Devi and Sulekha Sanyal woman bonding is employed as a strategy to deconstruct patriarchal discourse. They provide one with an infinitely significant reading experience by speaking about a camaraderie which has been successful in bringing about several socio-cultural changes. The reader is inspired to look back and to see the hard, backbreaking task of path making. They see the dusty, firm feet taking the first steps down the newly made, uneven mud path. Significantly, these novels also make the reader conscious about the present and of changes that still remain elusive.

Chapter V

Conclusion

A book which explores the thematic concerns and the narrative strategies of two regional writers of the past obviously faces certain questions. Why does the book focus on the texts of the past? Do they have any contemporary relevance? Do they speak to the contemporary reader in the same way they did to the reader at the point of time when they were written? Can the modern reader, who looks back through a distance of time, empathise with the authors and characters of a bygone era?

This book focuses on the texts of the past because of the author's firm conviction that they do have contemporary relevance and that they continue to speak to the contemporary reader. Any text, which defies temporal, cultural and linguistic boundaries, is eternally new and should be subjected to scrutiny in the light of ever-renewing cognizances.

"Books continue each other, in spite of our habit of judging them separately" observes Virginia Woolf. (*A Room of One's Own* 87) The four novels analyzed in this study, *Pratham Pratishruti*, *Subarnalatha*, *Bakulkatha,* and *Nabankur*, are the earliest resistance narratives written in an Indian regional language and thus they begin a dynamic tradition which continues to live into the present. As Ashapurna Devi says: "The shadow-dark waters in some secluded village overflow in the monsoon to join the river and gush forth in torrents. That same river rushes along, and, one day joins the ocean. We must never forget the initial flowing forth out of the shadows." (*First Promise* 2) These novels are the initial flowing forth of women's resistance. They document the condition of the kulin brahmin women in Bengal in transition between the old ways and the new, and depict their struggles to achieve authentic personhood. They have the status of classics now and even though they are embedded in a distant socio-cultural milieu, the feminist content in them functions as a unique correlative principle that cathects the timeless and the temporal.

The success of the texts which defy the boundaries of temporality depends upon their potential to enter into dialogic relationship with readers of different generations. Indira Chowdhury who translated *Pratham Pratishruti* dedicates the translation to three generations of women and acknowledges the intense and sustained fascination of three generations of women, her two grandmothers, mother and daughter, for the novel. Her grandmothers empathized with the protagonists of the trilogy while her mother sympathised with them. Her daughter's response is tinted with gratitude for the women who refused to weave their daughters' lives into preordained patterns and initiated the quest for viable alternatives. Thus these novels speak to different generations differently. But, very importantly, they do continue to speak.

Pratham Pratishruti, Subarnalatha, Bakulkatha, and *Nabankur* record the dreams and aspirations of women who were inmates of the dark antahpurams and motivate the women of the new generations to remember the heroic struggles of their foremothers who fought to help woman actualize her potential personhood. In Bakul's emotion-filled, silent promise to her dead mother Subarna, the author's voice, urging the reader to remember the past, can be heard.

> I will write your story anew, and tell my dazzling world the history of your silent suffering in darkness and ignorance. If this world does not want to hear it, if it treats your story with

> indifference, I shall know that we are still living a lie. The glitter of progress we've seen is no more than a reflection in a glass. Behind it, even today, is infinite darkness and endless deception. (*Subarnalatha* 209)

In the epilogue to *Agnisakshi*, Lalithambika Antharjanam, the most powerful namboothiri (brahmin) woman writer in Kerala, fervently hopes that her novel "will prove useful for the women of the new generations to remember their mothers and grandmothers . . . to realize and examine the bygone age's tears and dreams" (154). More importantly, she wants the women of the future generations to know the strength and courage with which the ordinary women of the past, who were incarcerated within the four walls of the antahpuram, met oppression.

The response of the contemporary world of readers and writers reveals its ever-renewing interest both in the women who fought to establish female subjectivity and the writers who made them subject of literary enquiry. In an interview with Savita Hiremath, which came out in *The New Indian Express* in February 20, 2007, Kiran Desai remembers the huge gifts bestowed upon her by her mother Anita Desai, in the form of the battles for space, time and money. She believes that it is the task of every young woman now writing in India to "remember the women who really struggled; and this work that we all so take for granted."

Writers like Ashapurna Devi and Sulekha Sanyal moulded the sensibility of our nation for many years to come. They belonged to the very small minority of privileged women because their families were comparatively more progressive. But they were perfectly aware of the fact that they were singular examples and so, instead of enjoying their difference, they felt the pain of the large majority of unprivileged women vicariously and gave language to their experience. As they belonged to the brahmin community, their narratives centred on the upper caste females' life, but they never kept the women of the other castes out of it. They succeeded in sowing the seeds of regeneration in the souls of the women of all castes and classes around them.

In her essay, "Mothers and Daughters in Bengal's Literary Space," Himani Bannerjee says:

> Our inheritance from our mothers, then, is not of property. . . . Instead, it is a longing for becoming, for a creation of ourselves, and an entitlement to discover, to recreate what surrounds us. This inheritance is a desire for sculpting a woman through the creative efforts of successive generations. This woman is sculpted by many lives of mothers and daughters, one taking up the task from the last one. (*Inventing Subjects* 180)

This description about the legacy of the mothers suits the two pioneering women writers perfectly. Their fiction announced, in both content and form, the work that was to follow.

The fact that these novels have succeeded in transcending cultural and linguistic boundaries also is validated by Jasodhara Bagchi. In the introduction to the English translation of *Pratham Pratishruti* [*The First Promise*], Bagchi records "the electrifying response from women across the world" (Foreword ix) to a paper on the novel, presented at an Interdisciplinary Women's Congress in Costa Rica. The reasons for the acceptance that defy cultural and linguistic boundaries and the "electrifying response" can be located in the writers' ability to anticipate modern sensibilities. Ellen Morgan, in her essay "Human Becoming," points out:

> It is not a myth that artists frequently also anticipate new sensibilities and are able to express, even if in fragmentary form, the substance and mood of cultural change before it comes into mass consciousness. . . . So it is not surprising to find that prior to the current women's movement, some novels were

> written by women who independently had come to many of the conclusions now being openly expressed. (276)

In the introduction to *Subarnalatha,* while evaluating Ashapurna Devi's contribution and achievements, Gopa Majumdar also observes that her novels were written long before feminism became a socio-political issue in India. "And she had never been exposed to western theories, as she had no access to English or foreign languages. Hence what we read here are Ashapurna's original thoughts, but based on her personal experience and analysis of women's place in society . . . yet it easily reaches out to all women across the seven seas." (viii) These observations are true in the case of Sanyal also.

These regional writers evoke, through cumulative portraits of the inmates of the antahpuram, memories of the great awakening which was a collective reality. Even though they draw from their indigenous cultural contexts, the universality of their concerns and resolutions are affirmed by the presence of similar concerns and thoughts in cross-cultural women's writing, as evidenced by Maya Angelou's *I Know Why the Caged Bird Sings, Gather Together in My Name* and Alice Walker's *Color Purple*. These western writers assert the deepening faith women writers place on the healing, empowering quality of female relationships. They situate their protagonists at the interstice between submission and resistance and record their struggles to reach subjecthood. Their texts thus bring out the similarity, which defies temporal and cultural divides, in the perceptions of the black American woman writer and the two Indian regional women writers, a similarity embedded in their faith in woman bonding. The writers refuse to naturalize victimization and so their protagonists do not stand with bowed head and lowered eyes. Their emotional intensity equals that of the female narrator in Maya Angelou's poem, "Still I Rise" who vehemently states:

> Out of the huts of history's shame I rise
> Up from a past that's rooted in pain I rise. . . .
> Leaving behind the nights of terror and fear I rise
> In to a day break that's wondrously clear (29-35)

The woman issue continues to be a volatile and contested discussion in the modern context, but obviously, it is no longer clothed in the initial form and vocabulary used by Devi and Sanyal. But they are extremely important in the scheme of women's writing in India because they were women who refused to allow their consciousness to be lulled by what Showalter calls "pseudo successes of token womanhood". (*Towards a Feminist Poetics* 407) Their views are futuristic and words prophetic when they discuss the concepts of women, nation and freedom.

The modern reader, who lives, thinks, watches and witnesses in a world where women have achieved a quantum of economic and legal stability, and where many material impulses to women's problem have receded from view, will benefit from the wise words reaching out from the past. Ashapurna Devi proudly recalls the great struggles of the Indian woman and agrees that she has traversed a hundred years in one generation, but according to her the work is not complete yet. "But the need for struggle doesn't end here. A lot has been done, yet much remains. It is not enough to demand legislations and have them passed but it is necessary to continue the struggle until we see the laws enforced." (*Indian Women* 21)

Both Ashapurna Devi and Sulekha Sanyal alert us to the several areas of life where woman still remains mute, invalid and invisible. Their protagonists declare in no uncertain terms that the country will not be free until the women are free. It should be remembered that one of the most vexed questions modern world repeatedly, insistently asks is about the futility of valorizing the political freedom of nations while the silenced and elided classes live in the peripheries.

Concluding *Of Woman Born*, Adrienne Rich passionately argues for the "need to imagine a world in which every woman is the presiding genius of her own body. In such a world women will truly create new life, bringing forth . . . the visions and the thinking, necessary to sustain, console and alter human existence". (285, 286) Looking back from twenty first century, we can confidently assert that these two regional women writers of India had dared to imagine such a world long ago.

Bibliography

Works Cited

Angelou, Maya. *And Still I Rise.* UK: Virago, 1986.

Antharjanam, Lalithambika. *Agnisakshi.* Trans. Vasanthi Sankaranarayanan. Thrissur: Kerala Sahitya Akademi, 1980.

Auerbach, Nina. *Communities of Women: An Idea in Fiction.* Massachusetts: Harvard UP, 1978.

Bagchi, Jasodhara. "Female Sexuality and Community in Jyotirmoyee Devi's *Epar Ganga Opar Ganga.*" *Embodiment: Essays on Gender and Identity*, ed. Meenakshi Thapan. Delhi: Oxford UP, 1997. 74-89.

Bannerjee, Himani. *Inventing Subjects.* New Delhi: Tulika Books, 2001.

Bose, Anima. "A Tribute: Ashapurna Devi." *The Book Review* 19.9 (Sept.1995) 22-23.

Carter, Angela. *The Bloody Chamber and Other Stories.* London: Penguin, 1981.

Castillejo, Irene Claremont De. *Knowing Woman: A Feminine Psychology.* Boston: Shambhala, 1997.

Caton, Louis F. "Romantic Struggles: The Bildungsroman and Mother-Daughter Bonding in Jamaica Kincaid's *Annie John.*" *MELUS* 21.3 (Autumn 1996): 125-142. Web.4 April 2008.

Chandra, Sudhir. *Enslaved Daughters: Colonialism, Law and Women's Rights.* Delhi: Oxford UP, 1998.

Chodorow, Nancy. *The Reproduction of Mothering: Psychoanalysis and the Sociology of Gender.* Berkeley: U of California Press, 1978.

——. *Feminism and Psychoanalytic Theory.* New Haven: Yale UP, 1989.

——. "The Psychodynamics of the Family". *The Second Wave: A Reader in Feminist Theory.* Ed. Linda Nicholson. New York: Routledge, 1997. 181-97.

Devi, Ashapurna. *First Promise.* Trans. Indira Chowdhury. New Delhi: Orient Longman, 2004.

——. *Subarnalatha.* Trans. Gopa Majumdar. Chennai: Macmillan, 1997.

——. *Bakulintekatha.* [Bakul's Story]. Trans. Prof. P. Madhavan Pillai. Thrissur: Current Books, 1988.

——. "Indian Women." *Indian Women. Myth and Reality*. Ed. Jasodhara Bagchi. Hyderabad: Sangam, 1995.19-23.

Devika, J. *En-gendering Individuals*. New Delhi: Orient Longman, 2007.

Donaldson, Laura. E. *Decolonising Feminisms: Race, Gender and Empire Building*. Chapel Hill N.C: U of North Carolina Press, 1992.

Fellman, Anita Clair. "Laura Ingalls Wilder and Rose Wilder Lane: The Politics of a Mother Daughter Relationship". *Signs*. 15.3, (Spring 1990): 535-561. Web. 4 April 2008.

Forbes, Geraldine. *Women in Modern India. The New Cambridge History of India.* IV.2. New York: Cambridge UP, 1998.

Friday, Nancy. *My Mother/My Self. The Daughter's Search for Identity.* New York: Dell, 1977.

Greene, Gayle and Coppelia Kahn, ed. *Making a Difference.* London: Routledge, 1988.

Hiremath, Savita "In a Room of Her Own". *New Indian Express*. 20 Feb 2007.

Hirsch, Marianne. "Mothers and Daughters". *Signs* 7.1 (Autumn 1981): 200-222.Web. 4 April 2008.

Hosseni, Khaled. *A Thousand Splendid Suns*. London: Bloomsbury, 2007.

Irigaray, Luce. *Thinking the Difference: For a Peaceful Revolution.* Trans. Karin Montin. London: Athlone, 1994.

Jung, Carl G. and Carl Kerenyi. *Essays on a Science of Mythology: The Myths of the Divine Child and the Mysteries of Eleusis.* New Jersey: Princeton UP, 1969.

Kane, Pandurang Vaman. *History of Dharmasastra: Ancient and Medieval Religious and Civil Law.* Vol. 2. Part I. Pune: Bhandarkar Oriental Research Institute, 1997.

Kristeva, Julia. *The Kristeva Reader.* Ed. Toril Moi. Oxford: Basic Blackwell, 1986.

——. *Desire in Language: A Semiotic Approach to Literature and Art.* Ed. Leon S. Roudiez. Trans. Thomas Gora, Alice Jardine & Leon S. Roudiez. Oxford: Basil Blackwell, 1981.

——. *Black Sun: Depression and Melancholia*. Trans. Leon S. Roudiez. New York: Columbia UP, 1989.

——. *Powers of Horror: An Essay on Abjection.* Trans. Leon S. Roudiez. New York: Columbia U P, 1982.

Leslie, Julia. *The Perfect Wife: The Orthodox Hindu Woman According to the Stridharmapaddhati of Tryambakayajvan*. Delhi: Oxford UP, 1989.

Morgan, Ellen. "Human Becoming: Form and Focus in the Neo-Feminist Novel." *Images of Women in Fiction: Feminist Perspectives.* Ed. Susan Coppelman Cornillon. Ohio: Popular, 1972.

O'Flaherty, Wendy Doniger. Trans. *The Laws of Manu.* London: Penguin, 1991.

Oliver, Kelly, ed. *Ethics, Politics and Difference in Julia Kristeva's Writing.* New York: Routledge, 1993.

Plath, Sylvia. "Stings." *The Norton Anthology of Literature by Women: The Tradition in English*, ed. Sandra M. Gilbert and Susan Gubar. NewYork: Norton, 1996. 2087.

Rich, Adrienne. *Of Woman Born: Motherhood as Experience and Institution.* New York: Norton, 1976.

Sanyal, Sulekha. *Nabankur: The Seedling's Tale.* 1956. Trans. Gauranga Chattopadhyay. Calcutta: Stree, 2001.

Saradamoni, K. *Matriliny Transformed: Family, Law and Ideology in Twentieth Century Travancore.* New Delhi: Sage, 1999.

Sarkar, Tanika. *Hindu Wife, Hindu Nation: Community, Religion and Cultural Nationalism.* Delhi: Permanent Black, 2001.

Showalter, Elaine. "Towards a Feminist Poetics." *Contemporary Criticism.* Ed. V.S. Seturaman. Chennai: Macmillan, 1989. 403-7.

Tharu, Susie and K. Lalitha, ed. *Women Writing in India 600 BC to the Present.* 2 Vols. New Delhi: Oxford UP, 1993.

Thrall, William Flint, Addison Hibbard and C. Hugh Holman. *A Handbook to Literature.* New York: Odyssey, 1960.

Walker, Michelle Boulous. *Philosophy and the Maternal Body.* London: Routledge, 1998.

Walsh, Judith E. "What Women Learned When Men Gave Them Advice: Rewriting Patriarchy in Late Nineteenth Century Bengal." *The Journal of Asian Studies* 56.3 (Aug 1997): 641-77. Web. 5 April 2008.

Watkins, Gloria. *Feminist Theory: From Margin to Center.* Cambridge, MA: South End, 1984.

Works Consulted

Abel, Elizabeth. " (E)Merging Identities: The Dynamics of Female Friendship in Contemporary Fiction by Women." *Signs* 6.3 (Spring 1981): 413-435. Web. 4 April 2008.

Ackerly, Brooke A. *Political Theory and Feminist Social Criticism.* Cambridge: Cambridge UP, 2000.

Aers, David. *Community, Gender, and Individual Identity.* London: Routledge, 1988.

Afshar, Haleh, ed. *Women, Work and Ideology in the Third World.* London: Tavistock, 1985.

Agarwal, S.P. *Women's Education in India: Present Status, Perspective Plan, Statistical Indicators with a Global View.* Vol. 3. New Delhi: Concept, 2001.

Agnes, Flavia. *Law and Gender Inequality: The Politics of Women's Rights in India.* New Delhi: Oxford U P, 2000.

Angelou, Maya. *I Know Why the Caged Bird Sings.* New York: Bantam, 1971.

——. *Gather Together in My Name.* London: Virago, 1985.

Aravamudan, Gita. *Voices in My Blood.* New Delhi: Sterling, 1990.

Armstrong, Isobal. *New Feminist Discourses.* London: Routledge, 1992.

Athavale, Parvathi. *Hindu Widow: An Autobiography.* Trans. Rev. Justin E. Abbot.1930. New Delhi: Reliance, 1986.

Bagchi, Jasodhara, ed. *The Changing Status of Women in West Bengal, 1970-2000: The Challenge Ahead.* New Delhi: Sage, 2005.

Bagwe, Anjali. *Of Woman Caste: The Experience of Gender in Rural India.* Calcutta: Stree, 1995.

Barr, Marleen. *Alien to Femininity: Speculative Fiction and Feminist Theory.* New York: Greenwood, 1987.

Bartky, Sandra Lee. *Femininity and Domination: Studies in Phenomenology of Oppression.* New York: Routledge, 1990.

Basu, Monmayee. *Hindu Women and Marriage Law: From Sacrament to Contract.* New Delhi: Oxford UP, 2001.

Basu, Srimati "The Bleeding Edge: Resistance as Strength and Paralysis," *Indian Journal of Gender Studies* 7.2 (July-Dec. 2000.): 185-202.

Baxi, Upendra and Bakhu Parekh, ed. *Crisis and Change in Contemporary India.* New Delhi: Sage, 1995.

Beauvoir, Simone de. *Memoirs of a Dutiful Daughter.* Trans. James Kirkup. London: Penguin, 1959.

Becker-Leckrone, Megan. *Julia Kristeva and Literary Theory.* New York: Palgrave Macmillan, 2005.

Belsey, Catherine and Jane Moore, ed. *The Feminist Reader: Essays in Gender and the Politics of Literary Criticism.* New York: Basil Blackwell, 1989.

Bhattacharya, Rinki, ed. *Janani-Mothers, Daughters, Motherhood.* New Delhi: Sage, 2006.

Bihari, Rasik "An Appraisal of Ashapurna Devi's Trilogy," *Indian Literature* 27.1 (Jan.-Feb. 1984): 35-54.

Biswas, Dipti Kumar. *Sociology of Major Bengali Novels*. Haryana: Academic, 1974.

Borthwick, Meridth. *The Changing Role of Women in Bengal, 1849-1905*. Princeton: Princeton UP, 1984.

Bose, Anima. "Ashapurna Devi: Perspective on a Bengali Novelist." *Indian Literature* 19.3 (May-June 1976): 80-95.

Branca, Patricia. *Silent Sisterhood: Middleclass Woman in the Victorian Home*. London: Croom Helm, 1975.

Brennan, Teresa, ed. *Feminism and Psychoanalysis*. London: Routledge, 1989.

Brown Miller, Susan. *Femininity*. London: Paladin Grafton, 1986.

Butler, Judith. *Gender Trouble: Feminism and the Subversion of Identity*. 1990. New York: Routledge, 2006.

Chakravarti, Uma. *Rewriting History: The Life and Times of Pandita Ramabai*. New Delhi: Kali for Women, 1998.

Chatterjee, Partha and Pradeep Jeganathan, ed. *Community, Gender and Violence*. Delhi: Permanent Black, 2000.

Chatterjee, Shoma A. *The Indian Women's Search for an Identity*. New Delhi: Vikas, 1997.

Chaudhuri, Supriya and Sajini Mukherji, ed. *Literature and Gender*. Chennai: Orient Longman, 2002.

Corbett, Jim. *The Second Jim Corbett Omnibus*. New Delhi: Oxford UP, 1991.

Crowley, Helen and Susan Himmelweit. *Knowing Women: Feminism and Knowledge*. Cambridge: Polity, 1992.

Das, J.L. "Ashapurna Devi." *The Indian P.E.N.* 44.9-10 (Sep.-Oct. 1978): 12-13.

Das, Subrata Kumar. "In Search of Sulekha Sanyal". *Daily Star* April 18, 2009. Web.11 June 2009. n.p.

Devi, Ashapurna. *Prathama Pratishruti*. Trans. P. Madhavan Pillai. Thrissur: Current Books, 1985.

——. *Subarnalatha*. Trans. P. Madhavan Pillai. Thrissur: Current Books, 1986.

——. *Aniyara Sangeetham* [Music in the Inner Spaces]. Trans. K. Radhakrishnan. Kottayam: D.C. Books, 1992.

——. "A Woman's Secret Treasures". Trans. Phyllis Granoff. *Journal of South Asian Literature* 21.2 (Summer / Fall 1986): n.p.

Dhawan, R.K. *Indian Women Novelists,* 3 Sets 18 Vols. New Delhi: Prestige, 1991-1995.

Dhruvarajan, Vanaja. *Hindu Woman and the Power of Ideology*. New Delhi: Vistaar, 1989.

Dinesh, Kamini, ed. *Between Spaces of Silence: Women Creative Writers*. New Delhi: Sterling, 1994.

Dube, Leela. *Anthropological Explorations in Gender: Intersecting Fields*. New Delhi. Sage, 2001.

——. *Women and Kinship*. New Delhi: Vistaar, 1997.

Embree, Ainslie T., ed. *Sources of Indian Tradition Vol. 1 From the Beginning to 1800*. Delhi: Penguin, 1991.

Etter-Lewis, Gwendolyn and Michele Foster, ed. *Unrelated Kin: Race and Gender in Women's Personal Narratives*. New York: Routledge, 1996.

Evans, Richard J. *Comrades and Sisters: Feminism, Socialism and Pacifism in Europe 1870-1945*. Sussex: Wheat Sheaf, 1987.

Gardiner, Judith Kegan. "A Wake for Mother: The Maternal Deathbed in Women's Fiction." *Feminist Studies* 4.2. (June 1978): 146-165. Web. 4 April 2008.

Ghosh, S.K. *Women in a Changing Society*. New Delhi: Ashish, 1984.

Goel, Savita. "Deconstructing Patriarchal Structures: Ashapurna Devi's *Pratham Pratishruti*." *Indian Women Writers: Critical Perspectives*, ed. Jayadip Sinh K. Dodiya and K.V. Surendran. New Delhi: Sarup, 1999. 163-69.

Gordon, Tuula. *Feminist Mothers*. London: Macmillan, 1990.

Grant, Judith. *Fundamental Feminism*. New York: Routledge, 1993. .

Gupta, Kamala. *Social Status of Hindu Woman in Northern India (1206-1707 AD)*. New Delhi: Inter India, 1987.

Hawley, John Stratton, ed. *Sati: The Blessing and the Curse*. New York: Oxford UP, 1994.

Hirsch, Marianne and Evelyn Fox Keller, ed. *Conflicts in Feminism*. New York: Routledge, 1990.

Hirsch, Marianne. *The Mother/Daughter Plot: Narrative Psychoanalysis, Feminism*. Bloomington: Indiana UP, 1989.

Irigaray, Luce. *I Love You*. Trans. Alison Martin. New York: Routledge, 1996.

——. *Democracy Begins Between Two*. Trans. Kirsteen Anderson. London: Athlone, 2000.

——. *Thinking the Difference: For a Peaceful Revolution*. Tran. Karin Montin. London: Athlone, 1994.

——. *To Speak is Never Neutral*. Trans. Gail Schwab. London: Continuum, 2002.

Jacobus, Mary. *First Things: The Maternal Imaginary in Literature, Art, and Psychoanalysis*. New York: Routledge, 1995.

Jha, Uma Shankar and Premlata Pujari, ed. *Indian Women Today. Tradition, Modernity and Challenge*. New Delhi: Kanishka, 1996.

Jolly-Wadhwa, Kanwar Sonali. *Gender: A Cross-Cultural Perspective.* New Delhi: Gyan, 2000.

Jones, Ann Rosalind "Julia Kristeva on Femininity: The Limits of a Semiotic Politics". *Feminist Review* 18 (Winter, 1984): 56-73 Web. 17 May 2007.

——. "Writing the Body: Toward an Understanding of L'Ecriture Feminine." *Feminist Studies* 7.2 (Summer, 1981): 247-263. Web. 17 May 2007.

Kaplan, Cora. *Sea Changes: Essays on Culture and Feminism.* London: Verso, 1986.

Karlekar, Malavika. *Voices from Within: Early Personal Narratives of Bengali Women.* Delhi: Oxford UP, 1993.

Kaul, Ranjana. "One's Own Patch of Sky". *The Book Review* 21.VIII (Aug.1997): 68.

Kaur, Iqbal. *Gender and Literature.* Delhi: B.R, 1992.

Kelkar, Meena and Deepti Gangavane, ed. *Feminism in Search of an Identity: The Indian Context*. Jaipur: Rawat, 2003.

Kirpal, Viney, ed. *The Girl Child in 20th century Indian Literature.* New Delhi: Sterling, 1992.

Klein, Ethel. *Gender Politics: From Consciousness to Mass Politics.* London: Harvard UP, 1984.

Kosambi, Meera. "Anandibai Joshi: Retrieving a Fragmented Feminist Image". *Economic and Political Weekly* 31.49 (Dec 7): 3189-97.

Krishnamurthy, J. *Women in Colonial India: Essays on Survival, Work and the State.* New Delhi: Oxford UP, 1989.

Krishnaraj, Maithreyi and Karuna Chanana, ed. *Gender and the Household Domain: Social and Cultural Dimensions.* New Delhi: Sage, 1989.

Krishnaraj, Maithreyi, *Women's Studies in India: Some Perspectives.* London: Sangam, 1986.

Kristeva, Julia. *Revolution in Poetic language* Trans. Margaret Waller. New York: Columbia U P, 1984.

Madsen, Deborah. *Feminist Theory and Literary Practice.* London: Pluto, 2000.

Malik, S.C, ed. *Dissent, Protest and Reform in Indian Civilisation.* Simla: Indian Institute of Advanced Study, 1977.

Marks, Elaine and Isabelle de Courtivron, ed. *New French Feminisms: An Anthology.* Sussex: Harvester, 1981.

Mc Afee, Noelle. *Julia Kristeva.* New York: Routledge, 2004.

Mc Naron, Toni A.H. *The Sister Bond: A Feminist View of a Timeless Connection.* New York: Pergamon, 1985.

Meaney, Geradine. *(Un)like Subjects: Women, Theory and Fiction.* London: Routledge, 1993.

Menon, Nivedita, ed. *Sexualities.* New Delhi: Women Unlimited, 2007.

Menski, Werner F. "Marital Expectations as Dramatized in Hindu Marriage Rituals." *Roles and Rituals for Hindu Women*, ed. Julia Leslie. Delhi: Motilal Banarasidas, 1992. 47-67.

Miles, Rosalind. *The Female Form: Women Writers and the Conquest of the Novel.* London: Routledge, 1990.

Moi, Toril. "Feminist Literary Criticism." *Modern Literary Theory: A Comparative Introduction*, ed. Ann Jefferson and David Robey. London: Batsford .1982. 204-21.

——. *Sex Gender and the Body.* New York: Oxford UP, 2005. .

——. *Sexual/Textual Politics.* London: Routledge, 2002.

Moitra, Shefali. *Feminist Thought: Androcentrism, Communication and Objectivity.* New Delhi: Munshiram Manoharlal, 2002.

Morgan, Robin. *Sisterhood is Global.* New York: Penguin, 1984.

Murty, Krishna T, ed. *Women in Colonial India: Essays on Survival, Work and State.* Delhi: Oxford UP, 1989.

Nabar, Vrinda. *Caste as Woman.* New Delhi: Penguin, 1995.

Natarajan. S. *A Century of Social Reform in India.* Bombay: Asia, 1962.

Nicholson, Linda, ed. *The Second Wave: A Reader in Feminist Theory.* New York: Routledge, 1997.

Nye, Andrea. "Woman Clothed with the Sun: Julia Kristeva and the Escape from/ to Language." *Signs* 12.4 (Summer 1987): 664-686. Web. 4 April 2008.

O'Flaherty, Wendy Doniger. *Women, Androgynes and Other Mythical Beasts.* Chicago: The U of Chicago P, 1980.

Olson, Karl. *Indian Philosophers and Postmodern Thinkers: Dialogues on the Margins of Culture.* New Delhi: Oxford UP, 2002.

Padia Chandrakala, ed. *Feminism, Tradition and Modernity.* Shimla: Indian Institute of Advanced Study, 2002.

Pandey, Rekha. *Women: From Subjection to Liberation.* Delhi: Mittal, 1989.

Pantel, Pauline Schmitt, ed. *A History of Women in the West: From Ancient Goddesses to Christian Saints.* Trans. Arthur Goldhammer. Massachusetts: Harward UP, 1992.

Parikh, Indira J. and Pulin K. Garg. *Indian Women: An Inner Dialogue.* New Delhi: Sage, 1989.

Phoenix Ann, Ann Woolett and Eva Lloyd, ed. *Motherhood: Meanings, Practices and Ideologies*. London: Sage, 1991.

Rabate, Jean-Michel. *Jacques Lacan: Psychoanalysis and the Subject of Literature*. New York: Palgrave, 2001.

Rabine, Leslie W. "Julia Kristeva: Semiotics and Women". *Pacific Coast Philology* 12. (Oct 1977): 41-49. Web. 17 May 2007.

Ramachandran, Vimla. "Fertility and Women's Autonomy in the Indian Family." *India International Centre Quarterly* (Winter 1996): 121-33.

Rao, Anupama. *Gender and Caste*. New Delhi: Women Unlimited, 2003.

Ray, Bharati. "Women of Bengal: Transformation in Ideas and Ideals, 1900-1947". *Social Scientist* 19. 5-6. (May-June 1991): 3-16.

Rich, Adrienne. *On Lies, Secrets and Silence: Selected Prose 1966-1978*. London: Virago, 1980.

Sangari, Kumkum. *Politics of the Possible: Essays on Gender, History, Narrative, Colonial English*. New Delhi: Tulika, 1999.

Sarkar, Sumit. *Writing Social History*. New Delhi: Oxford UP, 1997.

Sarkar, Tanika. "Politics and Women in Bengal—The Conditions and Meaning of Participation". *Women in Colonial India*, ed. T. Krishnamurty. Delhi: Oxford UP, 1989.

——. *Bengal 1928-1934: The Politics of Protest*. Delhi: Oxford UP, 1987.

——. "A Book of Her Own. A Life of Her Own: Autobiography of a Nineteenth Century Woman". *History Workshop Journal* 36. 35-65.

Sengupta, Mahasweta. "A Cultural Icon". *The Book Review* 28.9 (Sept. 2004): 35-36.

Shastri, Madhu. *Status of Hindu Women: A Study of Legislative Trends and Judicial Behaviour*. Jaipur: RBSA, 1990.

Showalter, Elaine, ed. *The New Feminist Criticism: Essays on Women, Literature and Theory*. New York: Pantheon, 1985.

Simons, Jon. *Contemporary Critical Theorists: From Lacan to Said*. New Delhi: Atlantic, 2004.

Sinha, Kabita. "Eswar Ke Eve". [Eve speaks to God]. *Women Writing in India*. Vol. 2, ed. Susie Tharu and K. Lalitha. New Delhi: Oxford UP, 1993. 330-32.

Sinha, Mrinalini. *Colonial Masculinity: The 'manly' Englishman and the 'effefiminate Bengali' in the Late Nineteenth Century*. New Delhi: Kali for Women, 1997.

Sivashankari. *Palangal* [Bridges]. Trans. K. Venugopal. Trichur: Current Books, 1997.

Smith, Anna. *Julia Kristeva: Readings of Exile and Estrangement*. London: Macmillan, 1996.

Sogani, Rajul. *The Hindu Widow in Indian Literature*. New Delhi: Oxford UP, 2002.

Spivak, Gayatri Chakravorty. "French Feminism Revisited: Ethics and Politics". *Feminists Theorize the Political*, ed. Judith Butler and Joan W. Scott. New York: Routledge, 1992. 54-81.

Srinivas, M.N. *Social Change in Modern India*. New Delhi: Orient Longman, 2001.

Swami, Siddhinathananda, trans. and ann. *Manusmriti* Thrissur: Sri Ramakrishna Math, 1993.

Tarlo, Emma. *Clothing Matters: Dress and Identity in India*. Chicago: U of Chicago Press, 1996.

Tikoo, Prithvi Nath. *Indian Women*. Delhi: B.R., 1985.

Todd, Janet. *Feminist Literary History: A Defence*. Cambridge: Polity, 1988.

Trebilcot, Joyce. *Mothering: Essays in Feminist Theory*. Maryland: Rowan and Littlefield, 1983.

West Kott, Marcia. "Mothers and Daughters in the World of the Father". *Frontiers: A Journal of Women Studies* 3.2 (Summer 1978): 16-21. Web 4 April 2008.

Woolf, Virginia. *A Room of One's Own*. London: Flamingo, 1994.

Index